Behin

Finding Hope When Life Leaves You Feeling Shattered

KELLIE BULLARD

Photos in this book were taken by Caitlin & Luke
Photography. Follow along on Instagram
@caitlinbachtold

ISBN: 979-8-8708-2750-6

PRAISES FOR *BEHIND MY SMILE*

"Kellie and I both share devastating stories of the profound pain that comes with losing a spouse. In her raw and honest telling of her experience in Behind My Smile: Finding Hope When Life Leaves You Feeling Shattered, her hard-won practical wisdom is a gift for anyone who has walked through a loss that changes everything and for those who are loving them. Grief inevitably enters all of our stories at some point. Kellie is living proof that if we allow God to use our pain for a deeper purpose and if we open up ourselves to the ways in which healing and hope are possible in the aftermath of our darkest days, He won't let a single tear go to waste because with Him, nothing is wasted. This book will encourage you to remember that and find hope in all the ways that life can leave us feeling shattered."

— Davey Blackburn
Ministry founder, author of *Nothing is Wasted: A True Story of Hope, Forgiveness, and Finding Purpose in Pain,* and host of the Nothing is Wasted Podcast

"Behind My Smile is an inspiring journey of redemption through grief and faith. Behind My Smile captures the experience of losing a loved one and life after loss. With grace and vulnerability, Kellie navigates the complexities of grief, offering solace and wisdom for those seeking comfort in their darkest moments. A testament to the enduring power of faith, this book is a beacon of hope for anyone grappling with loss."

— Ashely Bell
Founder of TALLBLONDEBELL

"Behind My Smile transcends the bounds of a memoir; it's a guiding map for all of us who have - or will one day experience - loss and profound grief. Kellie not only shares her lived experience but also offers a beacon of hope and purpose for those navigating their own 'unthinkable' circumstances."

— Manda Carpenter
Author of *Soul Care to Save Your Life*

DEDICATION

For my late husband, Alex, who always encouraged me to go after my dreams and believed in me more than I ever believed in myself.

For my kids, Halle and Krew, who have been my inspiration and driving factor behind it all.

For every reader who finds a piece of themselves within these pages.

TABLE OF CONTENTS

CHAPTER 1: JUST LIKE ANY OTHER NIGHT

"For I know the plans I have for you," declares the Lord "plans to prosper you and not to harm you, plans to give you hope and a future."

Jeremiah 29:11 (NIV)

Thursday, June 10th started just like any other day. I woke up around 4 am in a panic because our six week old son, Krew, slept through the night for the first time and I was in pain and ready to nurse him. Shortly after feeding Krew, my husband, Alex, got up and headed to the farm. He was a cattle farmer and the farm was about seven miles from our house. When Alex was eight years old, he watched his friend show cattle at the local 4H fair in town and he told his parents that he wanted to do that. So his dad told him to draw a picture of what he wanted, and his dad brought Alex's vision to life in their backyard. They started off small with only a few cows but gradually grew bigger and bigger every year. Alex was in the cattle industry to make and breed the cattle with the best genetics. He raised cows to be taken around the country and shown. He was very passionate about what he did. There was nothing more fitting as a job for Alex than being a cattle farmer.

The vet was coming that day so he needed to head in a little earlier than normal to get chores done and be ready. I woke our two year old daughter, Halle, up around 7 am and then we headed out for a walk. Halle had swimming lessons in the morning and then I dropped her off at daycare. I was on my maternity leave from teaching until August so I was still home with Krew.

Alex stopped by the house in the afternoon to switch vehicles. He had to get his truck to haul the water tank to the farm. We live out in the country and our well doesn't work, so we have a big 1300 gallon tank that Alex would have to fill up with water from the farm, or in town, and bring to our house. He had to do this a couple of times per week. He also needed his truck to drop seed bags off to his friend, Connor. They were finished planting and had some full bags of corn leftover that he was bringing back for a refund. He didn't want to put the full bags in another vehicle because they can spill a little bit. He came into the house to say hi to Krew and me. It was a really hot day, and Alex closed the blinds in the living room that I always left open to help keep the house cool.

Alex picked Halle up from daycare that day and took her out to the farm with him to finish chores. They stayed out there for a few hours and rode around in the ranger, looked at cows, and just played together. I was making homemade pizzas at home for dinner. I was trying out a cloud bread crust cheese pizza for myself and I knew Alex wouldn't want that, so I called him to ask what he wanted on his pizza. He responded with, "Baby, you know me! I'll eat anything. Whatever you put on there, I'll eat it. Surprise me!" A smile instantly came across my face and I laughed at him and told him I'd see him soon. I decided to make him a barbeque chicken pizza with onions and basil. Alexa was playing country music in the background while I was running around our small kitchen that felt extremely hot because the oven was on. I wanted dinner to be ready for them when they got home so I could be present as soon as they walked in the door. I knew Halle would be going to bed soon and I wanted the four of us to be able to have some time together. Krew was strapped on my chest in his baby carrier. He was a very fussy baby and wouldn't let anyone hold him besides me, not even Alex.

At dinner that night, Alex joked about how lucky I was to have found the best husband, and I joked with him about finding the best wife. We danced, laughed, and held each other in the kitchen. Our kitchen is barely big enough to have two adults in there at the same time. So having Alex, Halle, Krew strapped to my chest, and our dog, Gunner, running around in that tiny space, meant we were basically on top of each other. I opened a window to try to get some air flowing through the house since the oven had been on. Alexa was still playing country music, and Alex was so confident he knew all the correct words while he busted out singing them terribly wrong. This always made me laugh because it didn't matter how wrong he was, he was so confident in the words coming out of his mouth that he didn't even care when I would tease him for it. We talked about our dreams for our family and the kids. I remember him looking at me and saying that when one of our kids makes it big in sports, we were going to sell everything and follow them around to be at every game. We talked about what we thought each kid would be like when they got older. He started with Halle. I'll never forget, he looked me right in the eyes and said, "That girl is me. She is beautiful, funny, and smart. She's going to do something special. I don't know what it is, but she's going to do it." Then he proceeded to point at Krew and say, "That boy is you. He gets his emotions from you and your family. You're also just going to have to accept the fact that he is going to be a tank just like me, but he will thin out eventually." He told me that Halle was already a daddy's girl but Krew would be a mama's boy until he was at least 21, then he would come around to daddy. Alex was wearing his red Kankakee baseball t-shirt, gray Carhartt pants, work boots, and his worn Bullard Cattle Company hat. His shirt had black stains on it from laying on his back and working on his truck with his dad, and he smelled like the farm. I was wearing navy blue lounge shorts with lemons on them and a blue tie dye crewneck with the sleeves rolled up. Krew stayed on my chest in his wrap, and when Halle wasn't in Alex's arms, she was sitting at the counter eating her pizza.

After dinner, Alex put Halle to bed while I was holding Krew and trying to calm him down. Alex came downstairs, and we cleaned up the toys in the living room together. He asked me if I wanted more kids. Despite having a screaming six week old on my chest, I told him I did. We talked about when we wanted another one and plans for the house with our growing family. Then I sat down on the couch to read a book; Alex walked in the living room, slapped the back of the couch with his right hand and said, "Alright baby, I'm going to check the cows. I'll be back soon. I love you." Checking the cows was something Alex did every single night. They had cameras that he would pull up to watch, but when a cow was calving, he really had to be there to see exactly what was going on. He poured his heart and soul into those cows and wanted to make sure they were always taken care of. I told him I loved him and those would, unknowingly, be the last words I ever spoke to my husband.

Once Krew had settled down and fallen asleep, I heard a loud scream. It was more of a high pitched shriek really. There were two of them. It sounded like something you would hear in a horror movie. It instantly made me feel nervous and a little bit scared. I wished Alex was home to check everything out for me. I thought it might have been Halle, so I checked on her, but she was sound asleep. I didn't hear anything else, so I didn't think much of it and left it. I went into the kitchen to start cleaning up dinner and began loading the dishwasher.

At 9:13 pm, there was a knock on my mudroom door. It was my neighbor, and I immediately knew something was wrong. She asked me where Alex was. I told her that he went out to the farm to check cows. She then asked what he was driving. I told her he had the truck because he had to haul the water tank back. She took a deep breath and said, "Kellie, there's been a really bad accident and all we know is that it's a Bullard." I almost laughed because there was no way my Alex could've ever been in a car accident. He was the best driver and hauled loaded trailers across the country and through mountains. I immediately grabbed my phone and tried calling Alex, to which of course, he didn't answer. I then looked up his location which was about a quarter of a mile from our house, exactly where my neighbor said the accident happened.

I asked my neighbor to stay at the house with Halle because she was sleeping. I ran out the door with Krew still in his carrier on my chest and yelled for her husband to take me to the scene. My neighbor asked if she could keep Krew while I went up there, and I told her that he wouldn't go to her. I got on the ranger, and we were up at the scene not fifteen seconds later. I hopped off the ranger while it was slowing down but not completely stopped.

I ran towards what was left of his truck screaming, "That's his truck! Where is he?" There were so many people and soon after I got there I had police officers pushing me away saying, "You can't go back there. You need to calm down." People were in the field yelling questions at me asking if he was with anyone or alone. I kept asking people to please tell me something, anything, about what was going on. I remember pleading with an officer, "Please tell me what's going on! I have a two year old and a newborn. I need to know if my husband has a fighting chance." To which he told me, "I don't know." I remember thinking, where is the helicopter? Why isn't the ambulance moving?

It was around this time that Alex's parents arrived at the scene. They lived about ten minutes away from us. His dad, Paul, was driving his truck, and the road had already been blocked off by several police cars and emergency vehicles. I remember turning around and seeing headlights in the ditch just across the street. Paul drove right around all the emergency vehicles to get them there as quickly as possible. They came out of the truck the way I did, demanding to know where he was and what was going on. They received the same answers I had just ten minutes earlier.

I found myself standing in the middle of the road, holding Krew, staring at the headlights that were still lit up on his totaled, unrecognizable, truck. I swayed back and forth with the song Waymaker playing on repeat in my head.

Waymaker, miracle worker, promise keeper, light in the

darkness, my God, that is who You are.

I had not just heard this song anywhere. It wasn't a favorite that I would play on repeat in the car. It was just a gift that came to me in the form of a song from the Holy Spirit. It's like my body just knew Alex was gone even though no one would tell me anything. Nothing about the situation made any sense.

After some time, I went to yet another officer asking what was going on and where he was, and I got another response of, "I don't know." I looked him in the eyes and said, "Then find someone who does!" A first responder walked up during this conversation and said, "I think I can help. We did everything we could..." She kept talking but I couldn't tell you what she said because my world came to a complete halt. At that moment, it felt like the air had been sucked out of my lungs. I couldn't form words, I couldn't cry, I couldn't even scream. I walked away from her while Alex's mom hit her knees in the road shouting, "NO" and went back to the same spot I was standing in the middle of the road holding Krew, swaying back and forth, staring at the truck's headlights, with Waymaker on repeat in my head.

First responders spent the next thirty minutes or so working on him. I sat in the ranger and nursed Krew. I felt completely numb at this point and in denial. There was no way this could be my life. I refused to believe it until I saw him for myself, and I was furious that they kept making me wait. I remember people coming up to me, touching me and saying things but, I have no idea what they were saying. I just kept staring at his truck wondering what in the world happened. Shock had taken over my entire body, and I was so fixated on seeing him for myself because I didn't believe what the first responder had just told me. I remember looking to my left and seeing my selfless, kind, and loving husband being carried by several men in a black body bag and being placed onto a stretcher in the middle of the road. I immediately handed Krew to my friend who was the closest person to me and took off to go see him. A police officer held me back and told me the coroner would take me over to see him. The coroner came up and gave me Alex's wallet and asked where he was born. I answered his question, he kept talking, and I took off storming towards the stretcher. My father-in-law called after me, grabbed my hand, and said, "Kellie, I need you to be strong." I nodded my head and kept going while holding his rough hand. I knew that Paul was just trying to help prepare me for what I was about to see, but there was nothing that ever could. I wasn't going to stop until I saw him.

Then in a body bag on a stretcher in the middle of the road a quarter of a mile from our house, I saw a sight that no one should ever have to see. My twenty-seven year old husband who was so full of life, had so much personality, and could never sit still, was laying as still as a rock. I threw myself on top of him. I will never forget the feeling of laying on my husband's chest and not feeling him breathe. Or feeling his skin, that was usually so hot, being ice cold. Or seeing his right eye still slightly opened and thinking that they were wrong. Or seeing the countless bruises, cuts, and deformities visible on his body where there was once perfect skin. Or feeling what it felt like to kiss my husband's lips and not feel anything back. Or feeling the pads under his shirt that were used to try and restart his heart. There was no blood and his clothes weren't ripped anywhere. Seeing that sight, feeling the person I loved the most in the world helplessly laying there, completely still, I finally believed them.

It broke me in ways I can't even describe. I was uncontrollable yet couldn't move. I just wanted to stay there and hold him for as long as they would let me. He had eczema on the back of his arms, and I loved running my hands along it. I had my left hand on his right arm, my right hand on his face, and my head on his chest. After some time, I turned around to find a circle around me of all the first responders and police officers at the scene. I looked at them, through the flashing lights, and said, "Will you please keep him warm? He's so cold." They all just stared at me. My father-in-law eventually said, "They will, Kellie. They will."

I walked around the field aimlessly looking for what I thought was going to be a needle in a haystack: his phone. I looked up his phone's location on mine and it was somewhere in the field. I wasn't leaving until I was holding it in my own hands. I tried calling his phone repeatedly, hoping to hear it ringing, but I knew it was on vibrate and we wouldn't be able to hear it in the grass. I strained my ears, listening for any sound but all I could hear was silence. My neighbor eventually found his phone in the darkness and immediately gave it to me. His phone somehow felt as though it was going to hold answers to my questions, but it didn't.

Later that evening, I found out that the scream I had heard earlier while reading my book was the scream of the stranger who found my husband lying unconscious in the field and performed CPR on him until help came. I was sitting on the couch when I heard that scream. The line of vision from where I was sitting looks directly out onto the deck and into the distance. Had Alex not shut the blinds earlier in the day to keep the heat out, I would've seen the headlights, his headlights, flipping and tossing through the air in the dark.

The accident happened on a road that is considered busy in the country, not busy like in a city. There are only fields surrounding it. The accident took place on our neighbor's property. There are no cameras to go back and watch to try and figure out what happened. No one knows how long he was there before someone found him. No one knows what caused the accident itself. All we know is that it appeared to be an overcorrection gone wrong. He went off the road slightly towards the right onto the gravel shoulder for maybe a foot; in an effort to correct his mistake, everything went horribly wrong.

After finding his phone in the field, my sister came back home with me. I put Krew down and went to lay in Halle's crib with her while trying to keep my tears silent because I knew when our sweet girl woke up, her life was never going to be the same and she had no idea. Coming downstairs, I stepped on Gunner's long, light blue, plastic dog toy. It was his favorite toy to chew on and play fetch with inside the house because it didn't squeak. Stepping on that dog toy reminded my brain of something I had completely forgotten about. Our Blue Heeler, Gunner, was with Alex and also didn't survive the accident. Gunner went everywhere with Alex. He was a farm dog and Alex's little shadow.

This would be the first of many sleepless nights, lying wide awake in utter disbelief and shock that this was my life. I could not process what had just happened to me, let alone begin to fathom what life would be like from here on out. Quite frankly, I wasn't even sure I wanted to be around for it.

At twenty-six years old I wore many hats: daughter, sister, aunt, teacher, friend, wife, and mom. In the blink of an eye, "wife" turned into "widow" and "mom" became both "mom and dad."

CHAPTER 2: WHERE'S DADDY?

"Before I formed you in the womb I knew you, before you were born I set you apart."
Jeremiah 1:5 (NIV)

Alex and I weren't supposed to be outnumbered by kids yet. But here I was, outnumbered and left alone to raise our two beautiful babies. In the weeks that followed the accident, I was so numb. Numb to all the screaming, crying, whining–it didn't faze me because I was a shell of a human in survival mode every second of the day. Every second I had to remind myself how to breathe and how to talk. All I wanted to do was somehow try and manage to string those seconds together to get through the day.

I wore his clothes every day. Sometimes even the

same outfit for multiple days in a row. I didn't care as long as it was his. I don't remember ever brushing my hair or taking showers. I was bleeding profusely from grief. Not the type of bleeding one would experience during a period, but a constant, heavy flow that seemed to be my body's way of reacting. I would have the wind knocked out of me at any given moment, and then have to remind myself how to breathe all in the same minute. All I can remember is just sitting on the couch or the deck holding Krew like a zombie. People would talk to me and try to engage in conversations, and I just sat there. If Krew cried, I automatically tried to nurse him. It was like all I could do was stare out the window at the scene hoping to try and figure out what in the world happened.

I had no idea how to tell my two year old that last night was the last time she would ever get to see, hug, kiss, hold, or play with her daddy. I was twenty-six years old and didn't understand what had just happened, so how in the world could I expect my two year old to? Halle was a daddy's girl. She had him wrapped around her finger from the second she was born, and she knew exactly how to get whatever she wanted from him. They were the best of friends and seeing the joy on both of their faces when he would get home from work was always one of my favorite parts of the day. She would scream, "Daddy!" while running full speed over to him, and he would always pick her up, spin her around, and say, "Hi Snuggie! I missed you!"

I don't remember exactly when, but at some point

the following day, I told Halle that daddy went to be with Jesus in Heaven. She asked questions about what that meant, and I told her that it meant his life here on Earth had come to an end. We had this conversation multiple times each day throughout the next few months, and it was excruciating every single time. I had to introduce my two year old to the concept of death long before most parents would even consider doing so. I was given the impossible task of trying to explain the unexplainable. It was absolutely heart crushing. I knew she wouldn't truly understand the concept because how could she? We read a lot of books about heaven and grief every night before bed to try and help her better understand. There would be days that she would tell me, "Daddy's in heaven!" and shortly after that she would say, "Daddy's still at the farm doing chores!"

With Krew being so young, I knew I didn't have to worry about explaining what had happened to daddy, but I promised myself that he would know who his daddy was and how fiercely he loved him. Looking at pictures and videos is the best way for me to do this with him. The older he gets, the more he starts to question. I know I will have to go through it all again with Krew, just like I did with Halle.

I wanted to try my best to keep the kids in as much of a regular routine as possible. But this was almost impossible at times because I didn't have the capacity to do even the simplest of things any mother would do without thinking. I didn't realize when Halle's shoes were getting too small and she needed new ones. I didn't realize that I hadn't changed Krew's outfit in a day or two. I didn't realize that Halle hadn't been fed breakfast. I didn't care how long the TV had been on for. I forgot entirely what it meant to be a parent. It felt like an out of body experience, and there was nothing I could do or even think of to help myself.

Once my family headed back home and all the visitors slowed down, I sent Halle back to daycare and stayed home with Krew, like I would've done if Alex had still been there. Krew was just a newborn and still entirely dependent on me for every single thing. We would spend our days mostly sitting on the couch, in the exact spot I was the night of June 10th. I would hold him while sobbing uncontrollably because he was one of the two pieces of Alex I had left. Krew was still needing to be fed about every four hours, so sleep was nonexistent for me. When he would wake up in the middle of the night inconsolable, I was so angry that I didn't have Alex there to help me. Every diaper change. Every milestone. Every big and small moment in his life, his daddy would never see. It's exhausting having to grieve not only for myself, but for my husband and for my children, too. I grieve for all four of us every hour of the day: Alex missing out on both the beautiful and messy moments, the kids not being able to share those moments with their daddy, grieving what the kids do know from having a daddy for such a short period of time and also what they never will know, and for myself... trying to figure out how to do it on my own without him.

Halle was two years old at the time of the accident,

and we all know what they say about that age. We called Halle our sour patch kid, because one minute she would be sweet, and the next, you guessed it, she would be sour. Halle is extremely intuitive and was picking up on my pain and heartbreak. Every time the garage door opened she would say, "Daddy's home!" Every time the phone rang, she thought daddy was calling. Multiple times throughout the day, she would ask when daddy was coming home or if we could go see him. These moments of her innocence ripped my heart right out of my chest. Not only because daddy would never be coming home or calling again, but because I was going to have to keep explaining this time and time again.

We had begun potty training Halle a few months before, so you can imagine the major regression that she hit after the accident. Peeing on the floor happened more than peeing on the potty. The first few months when I would try to put Halle to bed, she would scream and cry because she thought when she woke up, I was going to be gone, too. So I would crawl into the crib with her while nursing Krew and wait until she fell asleep all while trying to keep my tears silent. I always had to tell her everything I was doing because she was afraid I was going to "get lost." She was beginning to experience separation anxiety. I would find her sitting alone with her head down crying because she missed daddy. She started to believe that Alex didn't miss her because he wasn't coming home. She was having more meltdowns everyday it seemed.

I began to notice my fuse getting shorter and shorter

with the kids, and my patience quickly went out the window. I could read all the research and books about how to help children cope with grief, but she was two years old and missed her daddy on a daily basis, and so did I. I didn't know how to manage my own emotions and grief, let alone try to navigate through Halle's.

Raising kids is hard with two parents, but Alex and I had found our rhythm and what worked for us. We noticed when the other needed a break and could step in. We could help each other deescalate a situation. We could be the voice of reason for each other. We had each other's backs and knew when to ask for help. Now, there was no help. There was no extra set of hands to help hold or prepare things. No extra eyes to watch them both and keep them out of trouble. No voice of reason to calm me down. No one was around to give me a break when I was reaching my breaking point. It was just me. Mommy was all my kids had.

I quickly learned to pick and choose my battles with the kids. Halle began to dress herself. She loved picking out her outfits and felt a sense of pride while doing it. I didn't care if she was wearing pajamas and crocs. As long as she was appropriately dressed, it wasn't worth the fight or the tears. It wasn't hurting anyone if she wore a princess dress out in public, so I let her. Her potty training went downhill, so instead of being frustrated and constantly cleaning up pee, I just let her wear a pull-up. It wasn't worth the fight, it wasn't hurting anyone or anything, and I knew that when she was ready, we could get back on track. Sharing became one of the biggest reasons for a meltdown with Halle. So we picked a few items of hers that were her "special" toys and she didn't have to share those specific toys with others. But her special toys had to stay in her room so we didn't have to worry about sharing them.

Motherhood became an entirely new world to me. I was relearning how to be a mom without my partner, and it definitely didn't come easy. I had to learn how to give myself an abundance of grace throughout every moment of the day, along with my kids. This was new for all of us, and we had to figure it out together. I was terrified of raising my kids on my own. I was scared I wouldn't be able to raise them to be kind, responsible, generous, and loving children by myself. I was scared that I would somehow screw them up. I was scared that I wouldn't make the right decisions or do something different from what Alex would've wanted. I became scared in a way I had never been before because I knew I couldn't be both mommy and daddy to our babies. I felt as though I had been thrown into the deep end and I had to decide whether I was going to sink or swim.

What helped me continue to string those seconds together to get to the end of the day was reminding myself that God specifically chose my kids and me for this. He chose me to guide and lead them through this tragedy, even though I would've never picked this path for myself. He chose me to be their mom. He chose me to teach them about Him. He chose me to raise and love them, even without Alex. He trusts me, He believes in me, and He is with me through it all.

One of the things that my sister said the night of the accident that always stuck out to me was, "God wasn't surprised by this." At first, I was angry hearing that but after I had time to really reflect and think about it, of course He knew. He knew the path of my life before I even lived it.

Losing my husband taught me just how little control we have in this life. Parenting without my husband taught me that I can't do it by myself. We all love to think that we know what's best for ourselves and know the direction we want our lives to go. And while I would like to submit my requests to God and have them delivered with no pain or suffering, that's just not how it works or what He promised. He knows my every need. He's already aware of what tomorrow will bring. And even when it doesn't feel like it, He's actively working things out for my good. All I had to do was have a little bit of faith and let him.

Trying to recognize the kids' grief and gauge where they are at is tricky. There's no script for people in our position. There's no telling when the questions from our kids will come. Sometimes, there's no way to know when their grief is affecting them until it's happening. It's heavy, but we are never alone. Let God help.

CHAPTER 3: I STILL REACH FOR MY PHONE TO CALL HIM

"For my thoughts are not your thoughts, neither are your ways my ways. As the heavens are higher than the earth so are my ways higher than your ways and my thoughts than your thoughts."
Isaiah 55: 8-9 (NIV)

As a first-time mom with Halle, I struggled with postpartum depression and anxiety. I found myself constantly worrying about her well-being every second of the day. I was losing sleep overthinking many things, but especially, if she was getting enough milk from me, and if she was gaining weight at a normal rate. People would make well-intended comments that she seemed too small, and this immediately made me feel defensive. I was already doing everything I could, including eating foods to increase my milk supply, staying hydrated, and even power pumping. What I failed to see at the time was that Halle had already depleted my freezer stash of milk before I even went back to work, and my supply was rapidly decreasing. I was in denial that I needed to supplement with formula, feeling embarrassed, ashamed, and guilty for not being able to provide solely breastmilk for my baby. No one in my family had to do that before. I tried to hold on as long as I could until I made the switch to formula and watched my once colic baby begin smiling, cooing, and sleeping through the night. While I grieved the reality that my baby girl needed formula and that my breastfeeding journey wasn't as smooth and seamless as I hoped it would be, it was necessary.

The stages of grief I experienced around how I fed my daughter came flooding back in a more intense way as I went through the five stages of grief over the loss of my husband. Denial, anger, bargaining, depression, and acceptance. These stages apply to losing a loved one, divorce, losing a job, losing a friend, receiving a diagnosis, infertility. No matter what we are grieving, we are told there are five stages to our grieving process.

While I have been through each of these stages during my never-ending grief journey, I can tell you, grief is not that tidy. We don't begin at the first stage of denial, work through it, never come back to it, and move on to the next stage. Grief never was and never will be linear nor will anyone be able to try and map it out for you. Because the truth is, grief is unique to each and every one of us who holds it. You may feel all five stages of grief at any given time no matter how long it's been. You may bounce back and forth between all five of these stages for the rest of your life. While I wish I could sit here and tell you that grief is a simple process that we can try and match an equation or algorithm with to plug in numbers and work through it, it's just not. It never will be an easy process that we can just neatly tie a bow around.

I remember people asking me as soon as two months later if I thought I was past the denial stage yet. My answer will probably forever be, no. I remember thinking that the one year mark was going to be the point in my grief journey where I was so sure Alex would just come back. I thought that if I could make it through a year without him, it would all be over. Because in our society, we have this ridiculous assumption that after a year, we should be done with the grieving process and moving on with our lives. I, unknowingly, bought into that assumption and thought my pain and sorrow would be done after a year. I thought the intense hurt and longing would just disappear and this cruel joke would finally be over. Surely Alex was just going to come back and so would life as I knew it. I just needed to make it through the first year, and then it would all be over. When in reality, that's just not how it works and while moving on isn't an option, moving forward is.

Denial is the invisible blanket that shields you from feeling almost anything at all for the first couple months up to the first year. It's the brain's way of protecting you from the pain. It's like your body is giving you the time to adjust to your new reality instead of it hitting you like a ton of bricks all at once. The numbness you experience is almost a blessing. I felt as though it was God's way of getting me through all the firsts I was about to experience. In a way, I felt like a robot. I remember at the visitation, standing up there for hours, I didn't feel a thing. At some point, it's like my body could no longer form tears. I was able to talk to the people coming through the line, and I remember comforting others instead of it being the other way around. People kept telling me how strong I was, but I had never felt more weak in my entire life.

I kept telling myself that Alex was just at a show, or at the farm and was going to be home later. He would crawl into bed, scratch my back, and hold me until we fell asleep. Eventually, after months of going to bed alone and waking up without him, my mind started to understand that he was actually gone. But my heart refused to accept that and kept wishing, hoping, and waiting for him to come home.

I still reach for my phone to call him. It used to happen multiple times throughout the day, now it only happens with something big. Like when Krew took his first steps or Halle started preschool. The first time Krew threw a baseball or Halle's first gymnastics class. When something exciting happens for me, he's the first one I want to talk to. There's no timeline with denial. In fact, I don't think it will ever fully go away for me because the more I talk with people who knew and loved him, they feel the same way. I still cannot believe that my kids have been alive longer without their daddy than they ever got with him. I can't believe that Krew will never truly know his dad or get to experience one of his famous hugs, talks, games, or advice. Or that Halle is growing up in this world without her earthly father. All of this will forever break my heart.

I remember every day having to break a habit and relearn how to do something new without him. Locking the doors at night before bed because he always did that. When there was a big spider in the house. When I couldn't get my necklace on, I'd call his name to do it for me. Running back in the house after getting the kids in the car to get my goodbye kiss and hear, "I love you" before I left for work. Pulling into the garage after a trip and having him waiting at the door to help unload and transfer the kids. Wanting to send him pictures or videos of the kids. Wanting to tell him the latest news around town. Wanting to ask him if we could go out for ice cream when he got home. Whenever one of these moments popped up (and they did numerous times during the day), it felt like a sucker punch to the gut all over again. There were, and still are, reminders everywhere that my husband is no longer here and that is still hard for me to accept.

When I think of denial, I don't think of myself telling people that Alex isn't gone, I think of myself becoming obsessive over every detail of the scene, the coroner's report, and the autopsy that haunted me and kept me up for nights on end. I walked every inch of the scene looking for some sort of clue. Blood on a leaf, a tree, the grass. Tire marks on the road. Scratches on trees. Indents in the grass of where he could've been found. I analyzed every single word in the autopsy. I Googled every word that I didn't understand. I looked up pictures of the types of injuries that were listed and found on my husband's body. I searched every inch of his totaled truck. Looking at all the broken glass, thrown papers, blown out windshield, broken tailgate, broken doors, flat tires. You name it, I thoroughly looked it over searching for a clue that we missed. We had to have missed something. I was desperate and searching for answers where I was never going to find any. I was in complete denial and thought I could somehow make myself feel better if I just found a way to have it all make sense.

Denial can take many different forms. Sometimes people keep themselves busy to try and avoid thinking about their loss. Some people use humor as a form of denial. Others procrastinate, isolate themselves, avoid certain things, abuse drugs or alcohol, or take care of others instead of taking care of themselves. Just like grief is unique to every person who holds it, each stage is also unique to how we handle our new reality. You work through grief in your own way and on your own terms. Drop the expectations that you think other people have for you. There is no timeline. Give yourself permission to fully feel however you need to.

I don't believe that living in denial after an earth shattering loss means living in the past. It simply means that we are continuing to carry our loved ones' memories with us and keeping them alive the only way we are now able. It's okay to *be* in denial about losing a loved one, a relationship ending, or finding out some life-altering news. That's all normal. We just can't *live* in the state of denial. At some point we have to accept that this is our God given assignment in life. Instead of asking all the troubling questions of "why me?" we need to shift our questions to "what does God want me to learn from this experience?" Dwelling on the why's will only take you down a rabbit hole and provides no true answers. We may never know why in this life. Giving this thought up isn't easy. I struggled because I felt I deserved an answer as to why all this pain was allowed in my life. But then I realized that even if I knew why or the answer to any of my why questions, it wouldn't bring me more peace… and it wouldn't bring Alex back.

When you pivot from your "why" to figure out what God wants you to learn, your perspective shifts. In our deepest valley of grief, we don't need explanations or reasons, we need healing. We need restoration. We need to know that God cares, that He's with us, that He knows something we don't. We need to know that our pain will not be for nothing.

I noticed this shift happened to me about five months after the accident. I realized that my time and energy was better spent honoring and loving Alex as best as I could with the time I've been given here. I needed to focus on raising our kids and healing as a family. Not dwelling on something that was a part of God's plan and completely out of my control. My obsessive behaviors stopped, and

I gave myself permission to ride out the waves of denial that would inevitably come. My thoughts and desires to know every detail about what happened seemed more important than they actually were. Figuring out my life will never bring me rest and even in the painful moments when I wish I knew what I can't know, rest is never found in trying to understand it all. Yet rest can be found because there is One who knows. He rules what I don't understand with my good in mind.

I still struggle with the thought of living the rest of my life without the man I married and made two beautiful children with. I still try to control the illusion of forever with him and now all it will never be. But, I'm learning that I never had ownership over Alex, just a shared existence for a part in each other's journey. You see, Alex was never mine to keep. I borrowed his love, his passion, his light, his joy, and his presence until it came time for him to go on without me. His time ended sooner than mine, and I had to give him back long before I was ready. But I know when my time comes, he will be the first face I see and what a beautiful welcome to eternity that will be.

CHAPTER 4: SLEEPLESS NIGHTS

"For I am convinced that neither death nor life, neither angels nor demons, neither the present nor the future, nor any powers, nor height nor depth, nor anything else in all creation, will be able to separate us from the love of God that is in Christ Jesus our Lord."
Romans 8:38-39 (NIV)

As soon as I got home from work, I would immediately change into Alex's clothes. Usually a t-shirt and his sweatpants. I would let the kids watch one show when we got home, so I could get a few things done around the house and unpack from work. Then we would play, eat dinner, do baths, and head to bed. I selfishly kept Krew sleeping in my room for too long. I wasn't ready to be completely alone at night just yet. He slept in a bassinet and then a pack 'n play next to my bed. Nights were always the hardest for me. It was when I was alone for the first time all day. No one needed me and I could think straight, even if it was only for a few moments. Nighttime was when I let myself feel it all. The hurt, anger, crippling sadness, paralyzing loneliness, and everything in between. When I would finally get into bed and put my phone down, I never expected to get a full night's sleep. But laying in bed alone, with a sound machine playing on the nightstand was my new found sense of peace. Even if I lay wide awake staring at the ceiling in my bedroom, it was my quiet, relaxing time that I considered sleep even though it wasn't. I needed this slow part in my day.

Then it seemed every night, I would be startled and woken up out of my daze by loud screams let out by Krew. His screams were piercing and seemed to cut through my beloved silence of the night. The darkness only seemed to amplify his cries, making them louder and more stressful. I would start by trying to give him his paci back, but that never worked. I would check his diaper, try to nurse him or warm up a bottle, re-swaddle him, walk around, or rock him. I tried everything I could think of to soothe him, but nothing ever seemed to work. He was crying, and I was crying. He was screaming, and I would find myself screaming. He was exhausted, and I was exhausted. As the minutes ticked by, I would begin to feel a sense of desperation creeping in. I would be holding Krew in my weak hands, with tears rolling down my cheeks, looking up and saying,

"Where are you, Alex? I need you!" My body would start shaking, and I was always scared that I wouldn't be able to hold him up and might drop him. I would always end up sitting down on the bed, the carpet in the living room, or the couch. These middle of the night wake ups with Krew were where I found myself getting the most angry. I remember desperately shouting above his cries, "What's wrong! What do you need, Krew? I don't know what you need!" As if my four month old could answer these questions to help me. I was longing for just a moment of peace and quiet so that I could catch my breath and recharge my battery to figure out what to do next. I was sleep deprived, in the thick of grief, and exhausted on every level, so when he was crying uncontrollably throughout the night, I couldn't seem to function in the way I remember being able to with Halle. With Halle, once I hit my breaking point, I could always wake Alex up, hand him the baby, and lay back down in bed. I didn't have to try and come up with solutions or have a baby screaming and clawing my face and chest with their fingernails. I could get a break whenever I needed it because he was there. But with Krew, I didn't get that luxury, and it made me angry. My brain felt like mush, and all I could do was cry with him while holding him and rocking us both back and forth. I was angry that I was left alone to do this, to do everything, by myself. I was angry that I didn't have my partner there to help me or give me a break. I was angry that I wasn't able to handle these situations with Krew in the way I did with Halle. Everything in my world was different and much harder now, and it made me angry.

Anger. We've all experienced the feeling before. I've been angry when someone has lied to me, when I miss something important, when I can't find something, when I feel disrespected by others— the list goes on and on. After I lost Alex, I noticed that the type of anger I was feeling was completely different from anything else I had ever experienced in my life. I also noticed that it was happening more frequently than it ever had before.

When my toddler would smack me because she wanted daddy, I got angry. When I watched Krew throw a ball across the room and Alex wasn't there to see it, I got angry. When both kids were melting down simultaneously, I was angry. When my toddler screamed that only daddy could get her out of the car, I got angry. When both kids were sick and clingy, I got angry. Waking up with a newborn all throughout the night, I got angry. It's in these moments I would feel my entire body physically tensing up, my heart rate escalating, my insides feeling like they were twisting, and I would look up with tears in my eyes questioning both God and Alex. I'm angry that this is my reality now. I'm angry that triggers come up on a daily basis, and often without warning. I'm angry that Krew doesn't ask about daddy because he doesn't know any different. I'm angry that I don't understand what happened. I'm angry that I have to drive past the scene every single time I leave the house. I'm angry that I can't get into the car without crying. I'm angry that he left me here alone to raise our kids. I'm angry that all the graves around him got 60+ years to live, and he was robbed of over half of that time. I'm angry that I told him hundreds of times that I couldn't live without him, yet here I am. I'm angry that Alex is in heaven, perfectly fine, with no pain or sorrow, and I am stuck here without him living in absolute misery. So, I would yell at him. I would scream and yell at him through the tears because I didn't know what else to do.

I have come to find that anger is a type of defense mechanism. It helped me feel more in control when I was feeling completely helpless and drowning in my grief. My anger was a release of energy for a loss that didn't make sense or seem fair. I had to find a way to work through the anger in a healthy way. For me, working out and diving into my Bible were what helped me the most. Working out was an outlet that helped remind me that I was in control of my body. And it was the only thing that reminded me of that for a long time. Working out didn't change my circumstances, nothing would, but I needed to feel something besides empty. I needed to push myself, and show myself that I could do hard things because everything that I used to do without even thinking, like breathing, eating, and laughing, felt so impossible. Even if I would cry throughout the entire workout, I would still feel better after finishing it and remember that I was in control of my body no matter how much it didn't appear that way.

Reading my devotionals and my Bible was the other helpful thing that I would do to help release anger when I could feel it pent up inside of me. I needed to be reminded of God's promises and know that He wants to help me through this journey. I begged God to help me. I would bring all my unfiltered questions to Him. I found that when I would do this, God seemed to be speaking directly to me. I would always get what I needed and felt more at peace for the rest of the day. I found myself making connections between why I was angry that day with the verses and stories that were put in front of me. I became more aware of His presence and was able to see how active He still was even when I felt He was radio silent.

I remember thinking one of the cruelest parts about this widowhood journey was being given another day. I would be so angry when I would wake up another day and have to live without him. It honestly felt like punishment for losing my husband. Everything did. I slowly became used to doing everything with the kids on my own, that I sometimes forgot this wasn't how it's supposed to be. And in those ongoing, recurring, never ending moments, I got angry. Angry for my kids, at Alex, and that I felt like I had been given a life I didn't even recognize most of the time. I had to actively choose not to let my bitterness swallow me whole.

I began to learn how to place these situations in God's hands instead of letting my anger control me. God is bigger than my feelings. I know that deep down, but in these certain moments, I lost sight of that truth. I got angry because my life didn't turn out the way I thought it would. It didn't go according to my plan. I'm angry because of what I feel I deserve even though I'm a flawed sinner who falls short every single day. God makes it very clear in the Bible that we will all go through sorrow and hardships in this life. He doesn't pick favorites. He doesn't distribute pain based on how badly we've sinned. He doesn't allow suffering without a purpose. And that can be a hard pill to swallow. There was nothing I could've done to have changed the outcome of losing my husband that hot summer night.

Fully surrendering your life and heart to God isn't a one and done type of deal. It's a constant battle full of fears and unknowns. But what I do know for sure is that God is working this out for my good and His glory. Something more beautiful than I could've ever imagined is in the works right this very moment.

Asking God my questions when I'm angry doesn't mean I don't trust Him. There's a difference between going to God with my questions and running away from God in my questions. My questions aren't motivated by defiance, instead they're motivated by genuine curiosity and a desire to better understand the purpose behind the pain that's been allowed in my life. I don't receive cut and dry answers to my questions, but I do receive reassurance that God has been with the kids and me this whole time. You can't deepen and foster relationships with anyone by just accepting everything and thinking that's what trust is. Go to Him. Push back, ask questions, yell, tell Him your fears and doubts and worries. He takes me in every time I get to that point and it always feels like my waves of anger are gently met with waves of grace. What I've learned is, I can't escape a valley. The only way out is through it. And the best way you walk through a valley is with the presence of God.

CHAPTER 5: TIME *DOESN'T* HEAL ALL WOUNDS

"Even though I walk through the valley of the shadow of death, I will fear no evil, for you are with me; your rod and your staff, they comfort me."
Psalm 23:4 (ESV)

I used to think that bargaining could only mean negotiating a deal with myself or God or some sort of higher power. Since my loss was sudden and unexpected, I wasn't given the time or space to try and make any sort of deal– it was over, and he was gone before I even had time to miss him or envision life without him. What I've come to know is that, like every other stage of grief, bargaining takes on many different forms. The way I found myself bargaining the most was being plagued by all of the *what if* questions. What if I had called him and talked to him on the phone while he drove home? What if Halle went with him to the farm like she had wanted to? What if we had friends over for dinner and he hadn't gone to the farm alone? What if he decided not to check the cows that night? What if he was driving a different vehicle? What if he left earlier or later to check cows? What if there were cameras on the road? I had hundreds of questions just like those consuming my mind at all hours of the day. These questions just further prove the limits of my control over the situation. I so desperately wanted to go back and try to change things in hopes that they would have a different outcome. I felt completely helpless that there was nothing I could've done or said to turn back time and get my husband back for our family.

Another major way I found myself in the bargaining stage was comparing my grief to others. *At least she got over 60 years of marriage with her husband. It's so much different for her since their kids were fully grown and out of the house when he passed away. They were divorced before he passed. He was much older than Alex was when he passed away. They weren't even married.* And then there was the comparison of grief that had nothing to do with the loss of a spouse, but life in general. *Divorce, infertility, not having a relationship with a family member or friend anymore, a heavy diagnosis, your physical or mental health, or even grieving the mom/dad/person you thought you would be.*

I kept thinking about how no one else lost Alex the way I did. Typing this out right now brings tears to my eyes because nobody will ever win except myself with that mindset. Everyone's grief is their own to hold and make space for. Maybe you keep thinking that everyone around you appears to have perfect marriages, or is able to conceive, or has great relationships with their loved ones, or seems to have motherhood all figured out. Just like a snowflake, no two people will ever have the same exact experience with their grief.

Death is inevitable in our world. At times, it may be easier to come to terms with death when it occurs in a way that feels like a natural part of life's progression. Other losses turn our world inside out with no warning. Just because someone else's loss is different than yours, doesn't make it any less painful. The common denominator is loss. Loss is loss and there's no threshold of pain you have to endure to prove how you're working through your grief.

This goes for anything in life, when we try to compare in a negative way or keep a scoreboard, we will always be the winner and the other people we are comparing ourselves to don't stand a chance. While these feelings are totally normal in grief, we can't sit in it for too long. These feelings can change at different times in life. Maybe you're waiting for your college acceptance letter while friends have already committed. Maybe you're the last friend to get engaged and all you see around you are married couples. Maybe you're waiting on your rainbow baby and pregnant women and newborns are everywhere. For me, it was seeing kids around Halle and Krew's age playing with their daddys. I had to remind myself that their win, their happiness, their current chapter in their life, was not my loss and couldn't be compared. I remind myself that my pain will not be wasted and will be made beautiful by God. I know I will be joining Alex again one day, and when I do it will be for eternity. To help combat comparison, I made lists of all the things I'm grateful for to help me look to the future with hope. This helped shift my perspective from horizontal, worldly things, to vertical, Godly things that will last, unlike my fleeting feelings and emotions.

Everyone who knew and loved Alex was affected by his loss. Every widow/widower who is left to live without the one person they vowed to be with for the rest of their lives carries an indescribable pain with them forever. It doesn't matter how old they were, how old their children were, how long they were married, it all hurts. By trying to compare my loss with others, I was only hurting myself. It only made me bitter and resentful. I realized that I had lost enough, and I didn't want to spend the rest of my time here bitter and resentful. I knew I had to change something to be better not only for myself but for my kids. There is enough space in this world for all of our love and all of our hurt, and we don't have to justify it to anyone. I learned the hard way that there is no hierarchy of grief. No two losses are ever the same. Each loss stands on its own and inflicts a unique kind of pain. What makes each loss so catastrophic is its devastating, cumulative, and irreversible effects.

Alex's absence touches every area of my life, and I am left haunted by the memories. At times I have felt almost desperate to find just one part of my life that was not affected by his presence just to find something, anything, that does not suffer from his death. I had become the ultimate victim in my own mind. I would think that no one has suffered as much as I have, no one will ever understand, and no one can offer me help that will last. No one will ever know the pain I have experienced because it is my own, just as I will never know the pain others have experienced.

When I met Alex, I had just turned 19 years old. We were both college kids whose biggest worry was which bar we were going to that night. We quickly became inseparable. Just two months after we officially started dating, May 16, 2014, Alex told me he loved me. We were talking on the phone. I was in the basement of my sorority house in Bloomington, and he was in his room at his apartment in Kankakee. He had a baseball game the next day but couldn't go to sleep until he knew I was home safe. I didn't say I love you back to him until six months later on November 27, 2014. I had never said that to anyone before, and I didn't want to say it until I was completely sure. He was the only man I had ever said those words to. My heart knew that I was in love with him long before my mind gave in and stopped trying to fight it. The pain from losing him felt like someone had a chokehold around my neck and I couldn't breathe. It felt like a constant punch to the gut to talk to anyone, go anywhere, or see anything. The familiar world I once knew was now so foreign and ruthless. Where I once was gently floating, I was now left drowning with no help in sight. This pain was raw and all consuming.

I tried my best to keep it together in front of my kids, but sometimes that was just impossible. Things they would say, things they would do, places we would go, it all reminded me of him and how desperately I wished he could see it all with us. I started having panic attacks daily. These typically happened every night after I would get the kids down for bed. I would go sit on the bathroom floor and become unconsolable. My heart rate skyrocketed, my insides were in a knot, I couldn't catch my breath no matter how hard I tried, I would be shaking while rocking back and forth on the cold wooden floor, and the tears were never ending. I would sit there until my eyes became so heavy that I couldn't keep them open anymore. This became my way of putting myself to sleep for a long time: crying so hard that my brain became mush, my head was pounding with a headache, and my eyes physically could not stay open. It was the only thing that worked for me to get just a few hours of sleep before Krew would wake up needing to eat.

I did this until sometime in September, so for about three months. My panic attacks and breakdowns started to become an unhealthy habit that was too comfortable. My therapist helped me make an appointment to go to see my doctor. My doctor knew both Alex and me very well. When I saw him, he cried with me, he sat and listened to everything I had to say without judgment, and over and over again stressed the importance of taking care of myself during this time. I remember him asking me if I had any thoughts about taking my own life and I'll never forget my response. I sat there in a long, floral pink maxi dress, squeezing used Kleenex in my hands, mascara lines running down my face, with tears dripping on my chest and said, "No, but if God wants me, I'm ready." I was not suicidal but, at the time, the pain was so intense that I didn't want to continue living without Alex in my life.

We talked at length about what would help me the most. He was trying to figure out if it would be more beneficial to start me on sleeping pills or anxiety/depression medicine. He decided to put me on a pill called Fluoxetine. He said this wouldn't make my sadness go away, but it would help to slow down the panic attacks and level them out so I wouldn't swing from the lowest of lows to a slight high and back again. He told me to take it at bedtime because it would help aid my sleep, which is generally when I had the panic attacks.

***

I'll never forget Thanksgiving day that first year, November 25, 2021. I woke up feeling no different than any other day since the accident. I fed the kids breakfast, played with them for a little bit until Krew's nap and then put him down. After getting Krew down for his nap, I did a workout and then showered. I got out of the shower, got Krew up from his nap and then with no warning, no build up, no obvious trigger, I had my first panic attack in front of the kids. I couldn't move or breathe. I couldn't change Krew's diaper or play with Halle. I couldn't even speak when the kids would ask me something. My legs physically could not hold me up and I fell to the carpet floor in the living room with my bath towel wrapped around my body. I was completely numb. After about twenty minutes of sitting there paralyzed, I called a friend to come over, hold me, get Halle dressed, change Krew's diaper, and take the kids to my in-laws house for Thanksgiving so I could recover. I immediately got in bed and slept for two hours.

I always knew that grief was a deep feeling of sadness, but I had no idea the giant toll it takes on the body, mind, spirit, and overall health and wellbeing. I thought grief was like a bad thunderstorm that only does damage during the storm, but grief is more like an atomic bomb that goes off every hour of the day destroying every single thing you knew. You're constantly living with the shrapnel buried deep into your sides and as soon as you get one part cleaned up, another bomb goes off and brings you a new mess to deal with.

Grief unleashes a full blown war with oneself from the inside out. Every part of my body felt it every hour of the day. I got sick more in the first five months than I had ever been in the previous five years. Physically, I had never felt more weak in my entire life. I would find myself shaking uncontrollably. I was bleeding all the time. It wasn't my period because I hadn't gotten that back after having Krew yet. I think it was my body's response to trauma and grief. Before I had a breakdown, I would always start bleeding heavily. It would flare up when I was about to have a panic attack. I would randomly throw up. Before big dates, holidays, or events, I always got some sort of sickness. My body felt like it was quitting on me. Mentally, I had no idea what was going on at all hours of the day. I would leave the house with two different shoes on, the kids would still be wearing their pajamas, and I remember always wondering how in the world I would get home because I was in such a fog. The term widow brain is used to describe the fogginess and complete disconnect that sets in after the death of a spouse. Let me tell you, it's a real thing. Emotionally I was a mess. I constantly felt the deep heartbreak and then if, by chance, I cracked a smile or laughed, I felt so incredibly guilty.

People always say that time heals all wounds, but I don't think that's true with grief. Time changes grief, but never heals it. What we do with the time we're given either helps us move towards healing or allows us to keep hurting more and more each day.

CHAPTER 6: GOD *WILL* GIVE YOU MORE THAN YOU CAN HANDLE

"Blessed are those who mourn, for they will be comforted."
Matthew 5:4 (NIV)

It's been just over twenty-seven months since I lost Alex, and while my head has come to understand that he isn't coming back, I'm not sure my heart ever will. I used to think that acceptance meant forgetting and moving on. Please hear me when I say, that is not possible! Anyone who has lost a loved one knows that you could never possibly forget the feeling of your stomach dropping when you received the news. We could never erase all the traumatic sights, sounds, touches, and smells. Those are forever ingrained in our memory no matter how badly we wish we could forget some of those things. Forgetting anything about the night our world forever changed isn't a possibility.

Moving on is also impossible with grief. You never move on from the person you lost, but you do learn how to move forward. I think the fifth stage of grief should be renamed to moving forward. To me, acceptance implies that you've come to terms with your loss. Personally, I haven't come to terms with losing Alex, but I've learned that this is my new reality. God still has me here for a reason, and I need to choose how I spend the rest of my days. It is permanent. There's no going back or changing the fact that he is no longer physically here with me.

I remember the first time I saw any sort of light shining through a crack of the darkest tunnel I had ever been in. It was about six months later, and someone offered to keep my kids overnight so I could have a night off. I went to a small bar with a few friends. That night I cried, looked for Alex, and talked about him every chance I got. But that night I also smiled, laughed, and felt the slightest bit human again. When the moments of joy came, I didn't try to immediately push them away and force myself to remember what I had lost. I gave myself the grace and permission to enjoy the company I was with and try to learn how to re-live in my new world.

Acceptance for me meant living my life *for* Alex since I no longer could live it *with* him. When memories come up of Alex, I feel them deeply, and remember them vividly. What we both were wearing, exactly where we were, our conversations, what he smelled like, running my fingers through his hair with his gel in— all of it. The memories sometimes bring tears to my eyes, but they no longer send me into crippling attacks. Other times those memories are met with a big smile. I am so grateful for the time I got with Alex and that he chose me to be his wife. I never want to forget those memories or all the joy they brought me.

When I miss him, I let myself feel that, too, but the attacks don't come nearly as often anymore. That's the price we pay for love. I would rather have loved and lost Alex than to never have loved him at all. Just because he isn't here anymore doesn't mean our love went with him. My love for him will never fade or go away.

Around six months later, I remember starting to become more present with the kids. Where I once was a numb, shell of a human living in survival mode going through the motions, I was now living more intentionally. My kids had already lost their daddy, so I refused to let them lose me, too. I noticed when their clothes or shoes were no longer fitting them. I could do more than just brush Halle's hair. I wanted to run around the living room and chase them. Their laughter, their hugs, their slobbery kisses, their little voices, their gentle touches, and their sweet snuggles kept me going and waking up every morning.

Getting out of bed seemed like a debilitating task most days. I didn't want to get up, and when I did, I was mentally and emotionally drained before the day even started. I remember the first time I woke up and my body didn't feel like a ton of bricks. I remember feeling light and grateful for another day instead of angry that I was given another one.

I started getting out of the house more. I didn't want to keep isolating myself. This only made things worse for myself and the kids. We needed to get out, and we needed to do things with other people.

I know for certain that Alex wants me to live my life. He was always trying to do something or go somewhere. I think this was a big part of the acceptance stage for me. Realizing the harsh reality that, despite grief, life goes on. It doesn't stop for you or anyone else. Reminding myself of the person that Alex was and the way he supported my decisions every day made it clear that he would still be supporting my decisions today. He was my biggest cheerleader and always pushed me to go for things even when I wasn't sure about it.

For me, the acceptance came once I let go of the idea of trying to figure it all out. What happened? How? Why? All of those questions that haunted me and kept me up for weeks on end, weren't serving me. I thought that if I could somehow create an answer I would be satisfied. I would feel different. It would make everything better. But the truth is, answers to any of those questions would never do any of that. It would never bring me more peace, and more importantly, it would never bring Alex back to me. I surrendered it all to God. I remember crying to Him saying, "Lord, I have no idea what you're doing but I trust you." That was probably the most honest, gut-wrenching, and relieving prayer I had ever prayed. It felt as though a weight had been lifted off my shoulders. I was trying to bear the weight of the world on my shoulders every second of every day, and it was crushing me to my core. I needed help. I needed Jesus.

Every day I was reading my devotional and my Bible without fail. I was exhausted and praying to God all throughout the day. But I had never said, "I trust you." It was like that was exactly what He was waiting to hear from me. He was waiting for me to release my burdens on Him and surrender my life for His glory. From that moment, I finally started to begin moving forward in my journey with hope. Not moving on. Not forgetting about Alex. Not loving him any less. Just trying to pick up all the messy pieces of my shattered life.

Have you ever heard the sayings, *God doesn't give you more than you can handle* or *God gives his toughest battles to his strongest soldiers?* I hated hearing those words because the truth was obvious: it was absolutely too much for me to handle. God didn't cause the accident, but He allowed it. This world is filled with people who are dealt more than they can handle. And, the Bible is, too.

The apostle Paul wrote:

We do not want you to be uninformed, brothers and sisters, about the troubles we experienced in the province of Asia. We were under great pressure, far beyond our ability to endure, so that we despaired of life itself. Indeed, we felt we had received the sentence of death. But this happened that we might not rely on ourselves but on God, who raises the dead. (2 Corinthians 1:8-9)

If we truly think that God won't give us more than we can handle, we are setting ourselves up to question God when the hard times come. Lysa TerKeurst said, "God doesn't expect us to handle the life altering pain we've been given. He doesn't want us to try and carry the entire weight of it, which we could never even begin to hold. He wants us to rely on and seek His strength, not our own."

In this life, we are all given circumstances that feel impossibly hard. Whether it be a death, a diagnosis, a sickness, the ending of a relationship, whatever it is, we all have a story. So yes, God will give us more than we can handle, but He doesn't expect us to handle it. He wants us to hand it over to Him and remember that He always has eventual good in mind.

CHAPTER 7: BILLS WON'T PAY THEMSELVES

"I have told you these things, so that in me you may have peace. In this world you will have trouble. But take heart! I have overcome the world."
John 16:33 (NIV)

Just a little over nine weeks after losing my husband I went back to teaching. I hadn't really left my house much that summer except to go to church or to my sister's house. Going anywhere gave me a lot of anxiety because I had no idea who I was going to see. I didn't go grocery shopping once that summer because I was terrified of who I would run into, what they would ask, and how I would react. Friends, family, neighbors, and people from church graciously did the shopping for me. They never asked what we needed, they just led with their hearts and provided for my family so generously. My life was still in the most tender stage; a smell, a song, a laugh, seeing couples together, getting gas, driving– it was all a trigger and I was barely holding myself together at home. During a time when nothing felt easy or predictable in my life, staying at home provided a sense of comfort and stability that I desperately needed.

I was a first grade teacher. As you may already know, six year olds are blunt. One Tuesday morning, I accidentally overslept and I threw my hair up in a bun that resembled a bird's nest on top of my head. As soon as one of my students saw me she said, "Whoa, Mrs. Bullard! What is wrong with your hair today?" Another time, a student asked me if I had showered recently when I had in fact showered that very morning. Just goes to show that they have absolutely no problem saying whatever it is that is on their minds. These types of things used to humble me and make me laugh. Comedy was a welcome relief when spending all day with a room full of 6-year-olds. But after the loss of Alex, their innocent comments and questions became another trigger simply because I was panic-stricken by the thought of one of them asking me what happened to my husband.

I remember expressing this concern to my therapist. She asked why that scared me. I told her because I didn't know how I would react. Would it send me over the edge and into a panic attack? Would I lose it and just break down crying in front of the entire class? What would I do if I needed to leave the room to have a minute to cry

and collect myself? The class couldn't be left alone while their teacher was a mess. She looked at me and said, "Let's play one of those scenarios out. How would you respond if a student asked you what happened to your husband?" I said, "I would tell them that he passed away in a car accident." She looked at me and said, "You did it. You don't have to justify anything else." It blew my mind how quickly and effortlessly she had just taken such a big anxiety ridden conversation and simplified it. I live in a small town and we all know that everyone knows everybody's business. I knew returning to work everyone knew I had just lost my husband, including the students, but I didn't know how their parents had approached it with them. Adults, most of the time, have the ability to think before they speak, but small children do not possess that quality.

Going to work was the one place I knew exactly who I could expect to see and when. It would be my co-workers and students. No random drop bys, no out of town visitors, no old friends, just those people. That gave me a sense of comfort. With our society being as grief illiterate as it is, my coworkers didn't ever really bring Alex up unless I was already crying. I would unknowingly walk into work with mascara tears dried on my face and the teacher in the classroom next to mine would carry on a conversation with me while simultaneously wiping the mascara dried tears off my face and giving me a hug.

I'll never forget November 10th. It was exactly five months after the accident. I hated the 10th of every month but this day felt different. There was a physical heaviness that I couldn't shake off. I got through reading groups in the morning, and then I just couldn't stop crying. I couldn't control myself or calm down. My body knew what day it was. Kathy, my classroom aide, looked at me and said, "Kellie, I know what day it is. I will cover for you and talk to our boss. Go home. Now." I remember feeling relieved that not only did she recognize the obvious grief written across my entire body, but she also recognized what day it was. Daycare was off that day and my mother in-law was at my house watching the kids for me. I cried the entire drive home. When I walked in my house, my mother in-law was folding laundry, Krew was down for his nap and Halle was watching TV. I looked at her with heavy eyes and said, "Would you mind just watching them a little bit longer so I can rest please?" I went into my room and collapsed. My body hit the bed, my weary eyes closed, and snotty Kleenex filled the sheets. I was out for a solid two hours.

Going back to work was a big decision for me. I didn't think I wanted to go back to work just yet. I really thought I should try and take a year off and get my feet back underneath me before going back. I wasn't even sure teaching was what I wanted to do anymore because everything seemed so pointless without Alex. I eventually came to the decision that going back to work would be good for me because I didn't know what I would do at home without a job. I felt like sitting at home, staring out my window at the place where my husband took his last breath wasn't going to help the kids or myself heal. Work would help the kids keep a consistent routine, they would be able to play with their friends at daycare, and it would bring a sense of normalcy back into my dismantled world. I called my boss about a month before going back to work. I was supposed to have a student teacher that year. I told him I was going to return and I was going to do my job, but nothing more. I wasn't going to bring work home, I couldn't have a student teacher, and my kids would remain my number one priority no matter what. I told him that as a solo parent, I would probably have to miss a lot of work to be with the kids and it would most likely be unpredictable. He was accepting and gracious. He told me he had someone on standby just in case the first day came and I couldn't handle it. Every single time I had to leave work for sick kids or grief attacking me, he let me go without a single question except for, "How can I help?" or "What do you need me to do?"

You see living in a small town with everyone knowing your business has its downfalls, but it also has its perks. Ironically, I was a teacher at Alex's former high school. Flanagan Grade School serves preschool through 12th grade students. My boss was Alex's basketball coach in high school. He knew and loved Alex before I ever did. Small towns come together in the fiercest way when tragedy strikes, and I am so grateful for that. Having an understanding and gracious employer was one of my main reasons for going back to work. I knew I wouldn't have been able to go back if I didn't have a principal who could understand I would need more days off than normal after losing my husband.

Adults have the ability to think before they speak, but that doesn't always mean they do it. I was the only employee of the school who was widowed. I was one of the youngest teachers, but the only one who had lost their spouse. Remember when I talked about widow's brain and leaving the house with two completely different shoes on? I went to work dressed like that. A coworker was the same size and ran to her house in town and grabbed me a pair of shoes to wear for the rest of the day. Coworkers teased me asking, "How could you leave the house like that? How did you not notice? They're not even the same type of shoe! Couldn't you feel the difference?" I laughed with them and said I had no idea how that happened, but I did. The kids and I were dressed and we were leaving for daycare and work on time. That's all that mattered in my brain. I checked to make sure the kids were wearing appropriate clothes and the same shoes, but I never looked at that for myself. I was alive and the kids were okay, what else could possibly matter? So instead of trying to explain to them how my brain was functioning at a new capacity and filled with fog every moment of every day, I laughed with them and said I don't know. I was jealous that they had no idea what I was going through. If they left the house with two different shoes, it would be funny and considered a "brain fart." When I did it, it was because my brain is forever altered and will never function the same way that it did before losing Alex.

At lunch, a bunch of us would sit together and eat

and talk about our day: school, things happening in our lives, our children, the latest update on Sam's house renovation. Sometimes, colleagues would vent about their husbands and I couldn't help but feel hurt. It felt like salt was being poured into my already-open wound. There were moments when a co-worker would make a joke about their spouse's life insurance, and it felt like a knife was twisting in my broken heart. Hearing someone speak about their sleepless nights reminded me of my own lack of rest, which only added to my distress.

When I went back to work, I hadn't slept through the night since June 9th, and even then I was waking up nursing a newborn. I would make every effort to try and get into bed around 10-11pm. I tried to have my phone off by midnight. I was always looking at pictures, videos, or reading through my text conversations with Alex. I usually fell asleep by 1 in the morning, and then Krew would be up a half hour later to eat. I would nurse him, burp him, change his diaper, and put him back to bed. Then I was usually back to sleep around 2-2:30 before my alarm would go off at 4:06 for me to start my day. I got up at this time to make sure I could read my devotional, workout, shower, and be ready by six to nurse Krew and start getting both kids ready for the day. I would go to work, pick up the kids from daycare, play with them, make dinner, give the kids baths, get them to bed, do laundry and dishes, clean up around the house, and then repeat it all over again the next day.

On the bright side, going back to work reminded me of the village I had around me. I would walk into work and see a small gift on my desk or a handwritten card in my mailbox. I would get a warm, meaningful hug from a coworker with tears from both of us and be reminded of how often the kids and I were being thought of and prayed for. For my birthday, my co-workers surprised me with a massage, bundt cakes, and jewelry. My aide ended up taking the kids for me two days a week after work. We would switch vehicles from work, and she would go pick up the kids from daycare and take them back to her house for a few hours so I could have a break by myself. I would use that time to grocery shop, clean, workout, read a book, and sometimes just sit and do nothing. It was needed, but it never would've happened if I hadn't gone back to work.

By the time I got home every weekday around 4pm, I was wiped and ready for a break. I kept waiting for Alex to walk in the house and be that relief for me. Adjusting to coming home without him, without any relief, was exhausting in ways I've never experienced before. I constantly felt weak, exhausted, and like I was never enough for anyone. In the beginning, going back to work was draining physically, emotionally, and mentally, but in the long run, it was good for me.

CHAPTER 8: THE STING OF REGRET, GUILT, AND SHAME

"Cast all your anxiety on him because he cares for you."
1 Peter 5:7 (NIV)

It was a Saturday. The kids and I made the drive up to my brother's house to celebrate my nephew's fourth birthday. Both of my kids have never been great in the car. If it's longer than a fifteen or twenty minute drive, there will be screaming and meltdowns. Even with a TV to watch movies, a basket with crayons and activities, blankets and special toys to play with, they never enjoy being in the car. I tied blankets together to create a makeshift claw to retrieve whatever they dropped and give it back to help avoid meltdowns. I always brought extra pacis for Krew that I would keep handy in case I wasn't able to reach them if they got dropped. I made sure to leave at nap time so that both kids would take a nap on the way up. It wasn't perfect, but both kids eventually fell asleep and got at least thirty minutes of rest or quiet time. We spent the day at my brother's house, and the kids had a blast with their cousins. I brought their pajamas to change into before we left, made sure everything was set up and ready for them in the car, and hoped they would fall asleep with the darkness on the ride home. The first forty minutes of the car ride were promising. The kids were watching TV but not screaming or whining, they were content, and so was I. Then in an instant both kids were overtired and simultaneously throwing tantrums. Their eyes, once gleaming with wonder, now brimmed with tears. Their cries pierced the air and quickly became unbearable. Any attempts at reasoning or soothing seemed futile. It's as if they were feeding off of one another's negative energy, leaving me feeling helpless and completely inadequate. All of the day's stresses and lack of sleep culminated in this moment, and I was struggling to keep it together. I found myself frayed at the edges, and quickly became unhinged. Exhaustion, frustration, and anger crept over me and then with a voice of thunder, I snapped. With tears in my eyes I shouted for them to, "Please stop screaming! I can't concentrate!" My kids recoiled, and the air was heavy with silence for a moment. Their cries didn't stop completely, but we were able to make it home. The only cure for their cries was my touch. We got home, went straight to my bedroom, and snuggled together with swollen eyes and rosy cheeks. Once I got the kids to bed and the winds of my turmoil subsided, I was left alone covered in shame and regret from my outburst. In the quiet moments that followed, I couldn't feel anything except for guilt.

Guilt after losing a spouse is a force so powerful, it's uncontrollable. This type of guilt isn't as noticeable on the outside as other parts of grief can be. This guilt reminds me of being in a chokehold. Once you're in the chokehold, it's like the rest of your body forgets what to do. You just flail your limbs around and try to make contact with the person who has the tight grip around your neck. It takes over instantly, relentlessly, with no signs of backing off.

Guilt manifests itself in so many different ways. The first type I noticed was the guilt for so many things that were not only unsaid, but said. The night he left, I had Krew on my chest in the baby carrier and when Alex walked out the door, we didn't give each other a kiss goodbye. This was something we always did, but never when he went to the farm to check cows because he was always home shortly after he left. That was the first chokehold.

The next one was scouring through every single text we had ever sent each other in our short seven and a half years of knowing each other. In college, I got mad at him when he went out when I couldn't. When we were first married, I would get mad at him when he left the cabinets open, didn't clear the time on the microwave, left dishes in the sink, wore his dirty work boots in the house, let his laundry pile up, and a million other little things. I was so quick to be critical of all the things he was doing wrong, that I didn't take the time to appreciate all the right he did on a daily basis as well. What we look for we will find. Chokehold.

We don't usually remember specific dates unless they are significant. If someone asked you what you did on October 19, 2021, you probably wouldn't be able to recall much unless something really great or really terrible had occurred, such as the birth of a child or the loss of a job. I remember exactly what happened on October 19, 2021 because it was the first time I drove in the car without crying after losing my husband. It was a Tuesday and when I realized what I had just done, I felt like something was wrong with me. Why did I not lose it all while driving that day? I had to drive past the scene every time I left my house. At that point, I was still counting the seconds it took me to get from my driveway to the scene. I kept thinking what in the world made that day any different from the 131 days before that? Chokehold.

After the accident, the first time I laughed or smiled, I felt an instant chokehold. How could I possibly laugh or smile about anything when my husband was gone? What was wrong with me? How could I possibly laugh or smile in a world that I didn't even recognize anymore?

I felt guilty for all the things that were unsaid. We didn't have life insurance. We didn't have funeral plans. We never talked about cremation versus burial. We talked about making a will once we were finished having kids, but we didn't get there in time.

I remember wishing that Alex would've come with a warning when I met him in 2013. I wanted it to say: "I will fight for you. I will love you. I will protect you and I will be your dream come true. But only for seven and a half years." If I had known, I would've never let him leave that night. I would've loved him harder and held him closer. I wouldn't have been annoyed by the laundry piles, open cabinets, or dishes in the sink. I would've made him put his phone down at the end of the night and just be with me. I would've kept taking the videos even when he told me to stop. I would've taken more pictures. I would've made sure we had more time together, just the two of us. I would've done a million things differently. Death has a way of making you rethink every single thing you've ever said and done. But I learned something really valuable here. That's the whole point! If we were in control and knew exactly what was going to happen and when, we wouldn't need God.

The guilt doesn't go away, but it does subside. It's not always as intense and raw as it feels in the beginning. I still have days where I feel a sense of guilt for everyday things I am doing, but it isn't like it used to be. The chokehold has become a feeling that is fleeting. It used to be a sensation that gripped me tightly, constricting my breath and making it hard for me to focus on anything else. However, as quickly as it comes, it fades away just as fast now. It can be triggered by a variety of things that can change on any given day, but I've realized that feeling guilty after the death of a loved one is completely normal and makes a lot of sense. Just because you feel guilty doesn't mean you are.

For me, my guilt centered around control. I crave routines and need structure. I had a plan for my life, and before the accident, it was taking place accordingly. Go to college, get married, have babies, I did all that. When I lost Alex, I was robbed of all of the plans we had together. There was no warning, there was no way of predicting this was going to happen, it just did. And everything I knew about order and structure was thrown out the window. If I didn't have something or someone to blame, I would have to accept the fact that I'm not in control of my life. Holding on to my guilt gave me a sense that I could somehow control or reverse the outcome.

Feeling guilty when you lose a loved one is inevitable and it's a terribly heavy burden to carry around. The guilt of surviving. Why am I still here and he's not? The answer to guilt is grace and how wonderful it is that God is overflowing with grace.

CHAPTER 9: HI, IT'S THE NEW ME

"And we know that in all things God works for the good of those who love him, who have been called according to his purpose."
Romans 8:28 (NIV)

As I got towards the end of my pregnancy with Halle, my doctor started to notice that she wasn't growing like she should be. I was going in twice a week for ultrasounds and nonstress tests to make sure everything was okay with her. Just before 38 weeks, Halle dropped below the tenth percentile in growth. My doctor explained that she had Intrauterine Growth Restriction (IUGR), and they needed to get her out as soon as possible. I was scheduled to be induced the next night. I always had this vision in my head of what my birth would look like. I thought my water would break at home, I would labor around the house for as long as possible, we would get to the hospital, and I would have a natural birth with zero complications. But that was far from what happened. They started the induction process around 7 pm by giving me a pill called Cytotec. My body was responding really well and the pain was manageable. Around 2 am things started to take a turn when Halle's heart rate drastically dropped off, and it took the doctors a minute or two to get it back. The closer my contractions were coming, the harder it was for her to handle them. I was stuck laying on my left side because if I moved, her heart rate dropped. They gave me a shot to stop my labor and strapped an oxygen mask on my face. After her heart rate dropped off for the third time, my doctor decided I needed to have a c-section. I felt cheated and ashamed by this experience. I felt like a failure as a mother before I even became one. I wasn't able to deliver my baby the way my body was created to. I suffered with postpartum depression for months after having Halle, and it took me years to process her birth. I have never looked at a child and wondered how they were brought into this world because it would never change how I felt about them. I had to grieve the birth I thought I was going to have, and it wasn't easy for me to do.

Just like with Halle's birth, grief is just one of those things you don't really understand until you've been through it. Once it's your love, your support system, your children's father, your future, and your entire world that's turned upside down in an instant, that's when you truly

get it. When it's you in the front row at a funeral, it creates a haunting memory that stays with you forever. Your perspective, your thoughts, your demeanor, it all changes. It's a whole new world you're living in without the one person you need and crave the most. Things that were once so easy and familiar are now foreign and traumatic. Your brain goes into full blown survival mode and you simply do whatever you need to in order to make it through the next day, medicate yourself to try and fall asleep, and then get up to do it all over again.

I was so naive and oblivious to the harsh world of grief before I lost Alex. I had lost my grandparents, my mom had a stillbirth with my little sister, and I had lost pets. While each of those losses stung and brought tears and pain, they were nothing like losing Alex. Those losses shook up my world for a few weeks; then it was back to life as usual. But with Alex, it felt like I was drowning every second of the day, for much longer than a few weeks, and there was no one around to throw me a life jacket. I used to have a perspective that most people my age had. I cared deeply about my family, and they were my everything. But I fully believed that while Alex and I were in the thick of being new parents, we would get "our time" together when the kids were grown up. We believed wholeheartedly that we had the rest of our lives to go, and our time together could wait. I had a worldly perspective. Now my perspective is completely different. I realize how short this life is that we are given. It is but a vapor that it is quickly fleeting. I have no idea when Jesus will call me home to be with Him, but I want to make sure that when I get there I hear, "Well done, good and faithful servant."

***

My grandma was the only other widow I knew at the time of the accident. I will never forget at my grandpa's funeral I saw my grandma looking around frantically and she said, "Where's Bob?" It absolutely crushed my heart to hear those words come out of her mouth because we all knew where he was, but she hadn't processed it yet. That's exactly how it feels. You are so accustomed to doing everything with your spouse. Reaching for them in the middle of the night after having a bad dream. Picking up the phone to call them during the day when you have something exciting to share. Waiting for their warm embrace after a long day of work. Going through your routines and having specific roles to play during them. Simply talking throughout the day. My brain was trying to place him in every situation. I was constantly looking for him everywhere. If he wasn't right next to me, then where was he? There were numerous times I would see the back of a tall, dark haired man with his build and think, "Oh good, there he is." Only to have the stranger turn around and be instantly reminded that Alex will never physically be here with me for the rest of my days. I had to train my brain to stop looking for him, stop picking up the phone to text or call him, stop waiting for him to walk through the door. Those were some of the most painful moments.

My outward behaviors had a drastic change. I didn't care about anything. Not in a bad way, but in a new way. I used to worry about what other people thought about me. I would try to carefully curate my words to make them sound just right. I was easily offended. I was quick to become defensive. I hated confrontation. I was such a people pleaser. I was very selfish in many ways and didn't understand many things about life in general. After the accident, I remember my siblings asking me how I handled a situation or what I said to someone and I would tell them, "Nothing. Bless and release." They were shocked because I would have never done that before. I just had so many bigger, more important things to worry about.

After the accident, I became very blunt, especially to those closest to me. I would say what was on my mind and not think twice about it. When my family was all staying at my house, my brother walked into the room wearing a sweatsuit. I looked at him and said, "What are you wearing? It looks like you're wearing something from Space Jam." I would've never said that outloud to him before. I didn't think before those words came out of my mouth. I had never expressed such candor before, as I always tried my best to avoid disappointing others.

While I became less filtered in other areas of my life, I was still able to maintain care for someone walking through grief. Something happens when you endure deep pain in your own life. You begin to see and understand other people's pain more. You can relate to them whether they experienced the same loss as you or not. You can understand their thought processes. Davey Blackburn described it perfectly in his devotional *Pain to Purpose*. He said, "You move along the spectrum from just having sympathy toward someone to experiencing empathy for them." I became very aware of all the pain and suffering around me, and in those situations I noticed an increase of empathy that I had never had before. I chose my words very carefully. I thought through what I wanted to say and made sure that when it came out, it would be received correctly. I was comfortable sitting in the silence because I knew that no matter what I said, it wouldn't change their circumstances. Instead of trying to tie their pain up with a neat bow, like I may have done before, I simply wanted to offer my presence and time to help comfort them and ease the heavy burden.

After the accident, I instantly felt like everything I did was put under a microscope and broadcasted. People were watching my every little move and talking about everything that I did or was going to do. This is a common theme with widows. You know when you're in school and a fight breaks out? People instantly rush over to form a circle around the fight happening trying to get a closer look. This was my life now. But instead of a fight, it was just my every move that was being inspected. People were watching me so closely to see how I was handling the tragedy I had been assigned to live out. I knew that I couldn't control what happened to me, but I could control how I responded to it.

I immediately became a third or fifth wheel anytime I was with friends. Everyone had their significant other, and then I was just there by myself. I hated leaving my house for many reasons, but this was another big one. I felt left out even when I was surrounded by people who loved me. It was just another reminder that Alex wasn't here anymore.

Anytime I would see a family with kids around my kids' age, I would instantly feel jealous. Jealous that those kids got both their mommy and daddy to love, cherish, and raise them, and my kids didn't. When people would share their kids' big milestones and I would see the pictures with mommy and daddy in them, it hurt my heart. It was so hard to watch my friends, family members, and even strangers being the best daddy to their babies and playing with them knowing that my kids will never get that again with their daddy.

People looked at me differently when they would see me out in public. It was a slight look down, sad eyes, soft smile, my heart is breaking with you type of look. I would catch them looking at my hand to see if I still had my ring on my finger, too.

The aftermath of a death brings about a cascade of losses beyond the primary one, and they often come in many forms and sizes. I came to find out that this was called secondary losses. I had never even heard of that before. As I learned more about secondary losses, I realized there were triggers that came up all the time for me. Things I had never noticed or even thought about before would suddenly send me spiraling. It's important to recognize that it is never just one loss when someone dies.

I lost my sense of identity, my confidence, my sense of normal, my general sense of security, our family traditions, my financials, my dreams, my friends, my support system, my innocence, my working memory, my parenting partner. I would never be a passenger in our car again. Whenever I had to fill out paperwork and would get to the section where I have to put down my emergency contact information or my marital status, I froze.

I remember praying and asking God to please help me steward this pain. I begged Him to somehow let me help just one person. This pain was too great for me to bear and I needed to use it to help someone or I would lose my mind. So, I had a choice to make. I could either slap on a happy face and pretend like I was fine. Or, I could open my heart up and show people every little thing I was feeling and just how truly brutal and exhausting this whole grief thing really is. I was so unaware of what grief was before losing Alex that I knew I had to use my experience to help our grief illiterate world learn about what it actually is, instead of what we make it out to be. By doing this, I found that it was the beginning of my redemption in my pain. Sharing my journey, the raw, unfiltered, hard moments, was helpful for me and I quickly realized that it was helpful for others as well. You see, we all think that we are alone in our pain and try to hide it from others in fear of being a burden. When in reality, there is always someone else out there who feels exactly the same way you do and just doesn't know how to express it. God could be using your pain to help others walk through their pain and hardships right now.

By embracing the new version of myself that has emerged since becoming a widow, I can connect with, serve, and care for others who I never would have related with prior.

CHAPTER 10: X'S IN THE SKY

"Have I not commanded you? Be strong and courageous. Do not be afraid; do not be discouraged, for the Lord your God will be with you wherever you go."
Joshua 1:9 (NIV)

Once I felt ready, I started cleaning out closets. Not our bedroom closet with his clothes, but random ones around the house that we had thrown stuff in and forgotten about. I was in the upstairs bedroom that used to be our room, and in the closet I found a note Alex had written to me. It didn't make any sense that the note would be in that closet because I kept all of my notes from him in the same place on my nightstand. When I opened the note up, in the middle of the page, in a purple pen, all capital letters he had written, IT'S GOD'S PLAN. Then I was going through the closet in the living room where there was a bunch of stuff of ours from college. There were some of Alex's old jerseys and shirts that he used to wear during cattle shows that no longer fit him. I randomly pulled on two hangers to spread them apart and the back of one of his shirts had "here I am right where I belong" written on it. I had never seen that shirt before, but it felt like the exact time I was supposed to find it. Both of those instances sent full body chills running through my body. Despite tears streaming down my face, I couldn't help but smile. It felt as if I was completely surrounded by one of Alex's famous warm, loving, tender hugs. During my darkest days, these fleeting moments were glimmers to me.

Glimmers are the moments in a day that spark a sense of joy and wellbeing. I was living in a world covered in triggers, and I desperately needed those glimmers. Immediately after the accident, I wanted obvious, undeniable signs from Alex to smack me in the face. I wanted a plane to fly over my house holding a sign that said, 'I am so proud of you. I love you.' I wanted the clouds to spell out his name. I wanted him to be in my dreams so I could hear his voice again. I wanted out-of-this-world signs.

Now as you may have already guessed, I didn't get any of those things. But I did get glimmers. From the second I lost Alex, everything looked different, but the sky was the main thing that stood out to me. It felt different because the person I loved more than anything in this world was up there. I would search for the clouds to spell out his name, I would never see an A, L, or an E, but I kept seeing Xs in the sky. At first this drove me crazy, but then I found myself noticing the Xs in the sky when I needed them most. I started sharing pictures of the Xs, and pretty soon people began relating Xs in the sky with Alex and me. I have gotten pictures from all over the world of big beautiful Xs in the sky. I have even gotten pictures from pilots flying their planes in the sky and sending me the Xs they see from their point of view. It became a sign for me, a little God wink, that Alex was more than okay and was proud of me. Even when I didn't see them myself, someone would share their X with me.

Another sign from the sky was the sunrise and the sunset every day. We live out in the country and have a front row seat to an incredible view of both the sunrise and sunset. Sunset was one of Alex's favorite times of the day. We loved being out on the deck and watching the sun go down together even if only for a few minutes. When I look at the sky now, it seems so different. I never realized how magnificent it truly was. I could appreciate nature and a good sunset, but it never meant anything to me. Now, I take it as a sign from Alex and just another reminder of how powerful and gracious our God truly is.

One night while a friend had the kids for me, I got home from grocery shopping and the sky looked so beautiful. I decided the groceries could wait because I wanted to take in the beautiful sunset before it was gone.

I sat on the cattle gate in our backyard, talked to Alex and cried. I noticed something in the sky I had never seen before. I saw what I called a peekaboo rainbow in the sky in the opening between some clouds. I thought I was actually losing my mind. I asked about it and found out that the peekaboo rainbow I saw had a name, a sundog. The more I observed the sky, the more features I noticed that I had never seen before. I remember on June 10, 2022, the one year anniversary of Alex's passing I saw what appeared to be a circular rainbow, a halo, around the sun. I was so fascinated by it. I noticed rainbows of all kinds more now than ever before. They always remind me of the story of Noah and how God placed a rainbow in the sky as a sign of his promise. It always feels like a reminder of His promises when I see them now.

Less than three weeks after losing Alex, I was driving home from dinner at a friend's house, and I looked up to see a tree that was shaped like a heart. I had driven on this road hundreds of times before and never noticed it. The sky was picture perfect and the song *Even Though I'm Leaving* by Luke Combs was playing. For the past twenty days I had been desperately trying to make anything a sign from Alex but this felt like it actually was one. I look at that tree every single time I drive by it now and smile. I realized that as soon as I got up over the hill where the accident took place, I could see that heart shaped tree from my road. Even in the winter when the tree loses its leaves, it still keeps its shape.

Even though I felt connected to Alex through signs in

nature, I was getting frustrated because I would ask God every night to please let Alex visit me in my dreams, and he never did. People had sent me messages to tell me about Alex visiting them in their dreams, and it frustrated me at first because I just wanted him to come to me in mine. On July 13, 2021, I had my first dream with Alex in it and I experienced a moment of complete and total peace. We were in our living room and Alex was laying on the carpet (as he usually preferred to do) playing with Halle and Gunner. I was sitting on the couch in my usual spot holding Krew. All of the sudden, Gunner and the kids just disappeared, and I was laying on the floor with Alex. I laid my head on his chest and he held me so tight. Neither one of us said a word. We just held each other. Then he started to get up and though it wasn't audible, he told me he needed to go to the farm to check cows. I begged him to just lay with me for a couple minutes longer (this also happened all the time in real life), but he said it couldn't wait and then he was gone and so was the moment of peace my heart had felt. It's been over two years since I've lost him, and I have had three dreams with him in it. That's it. In every single one of the dreams, he never talks but I always know exactly what he's saying. Those three times he has come to me in a dream, my heart feels completely at peace even knowing it's only a dream.

***

When covid shut everything down, I got into running. I became pregnant with Krew a few months after that and I remember telling Alex I wanted to run a marathon someday, but I would need to start with a half. He told me I didn't need to do a half. I could absolutely do a full marathon. Then he proceeded to tell me that he wasn't going to do it with me, but he would be cheering me on the whole way. It wasn't until a year after the accident that I started training for my first ever marathon. Every weekend for my long runs, my friend would come watch the kids for me and during those long runs, I would feel his presence, his support, and his encouragement. I don't know how to explain it but the feeling was overwhelming. Then on my runs a song would come on that would instantly transport me back to a memory with him playing or singing that song. Or a song by one of his favorite artists would come on and it's funny how even the smallest things can bring me right back to a specific moment in time no matter how long it's been.

Halle also showed signs that she experienced Alex's presence, as well. A few months after the accident, Halle would point to random, blank spots around the house, not pictures, and say, "There's my daddy!" I would always ask her where he was and what he was doing. She would just keep pointing and then tell me he's with the cows, or eating, or going to the bathroom. I know that Alex wasn't there and she was just remembering times from when he was, but my heart needed all the wins it could get. I would never turn down an opportunity to talk about daddy and what we thought he might be doing.

A lot of people have heard of butterflies, cardinals, and even feathers being some of the most popular signs from their loved ones after death. Everyone's different and feels their own signs as a way of connecting with their loved one. I never believed in any of these things before. I thought people who did were a little crazy and honestly it sounded naive. But I realize now that we just need some hope. And if hope comes from a rainbow, a sunset, a song, or a bird, then so be it. These glimmers are constant reminders of how God cares for us and He is present with us in our pain. In my season of desperation, these glimmers sustained me. God is always big enough to show up if we just ask.

CHAPTER 11: DEATH REVEALS WHO YOUR TRUE FRIENDS ARE

"If it is possible, as far as it depends on you, live at peace with everyone."
Romans 12:18 (NIV)

When I finally caught my breath after his funeral, I realized that there were many people who didn't even show up. Friends who I had known for five to ten years didn't come or even text me the day of Alex's funeral, make an effort to come see us that summer, or send a simple check-in text throughout the years. At a time when I felt completely alone, these instances only served to highlight my isolation even more. I began to wonder how I could possibly feel more connected to strangers on the internet who I had never met before in person, than with friends I had known for years.

I wasn't prepared for how much grief changes people— whether for better or worse. Every single relationship I had— with friends, family, colleagues, my in-laws... even strangers, all changed. Some friends who I was sure would be there for me weren't. Some people, family included, that I expected to be high up on the list of people to walk through grief with me because of how close our relationship was before the accident, were actually lowest on the list of people to walk through grief with me. It hurt and it still does.

While some friends shied away from me in my grief, my family and my church rallied hard for me and still do to this day. My family immediately arrived at my house. They took turns sleeping with me so I didn't have to sleep alone. They took care of and played with the kids. They gave both kids their baths and got them ready for bed by putting on their pajamas and brushing their teeth. They made meals with protein and vegetables to help keep me fueled. They refilled my water bottle every time it was even close to being empty and gave me Body Armors to help keep my milk supply up. They went to the grocery store whenever I needed more milk for Halle or pancakes for breakfast. They would take the kids on walks down to the pond in the backyard, play hide and seek, and chase them around in a game of tag. Anything I needed, I knew they were there and would provide. However, my family is spread out across the country. My parents live in Florida. My sister (who is also my very best friend) lives in Tennessee. My brother lives in California, and my oldest brother lives in the suburbs of Chicago. Even though we are scattered throughout the U.S., my sister basically lived with us for the first month after Alex passed. At the time, they lived an hour away. She would wait for her husband to get done with work for the day, kiss her three year old daughter and almost two year old son goodnight, and drive all of the way over just to come help me get my kids to bed. Sometimes she even brought her kids with her so that they could be here for the entire day. She packed for all of them and adjusted naps and bedtime routines to work at my house. Every time she was here, she was doing laundry, cleaning up around the house, organizing things, cooking meals, and handling thank you cards on my behalf. My brother who lives about an hour and a half away, would come down once a week to help me with the kids and get them to bed. My parents would come back whenever I needed them and helped financially. My best friend, who lives just four miles away, was with me all day until the kids would go down for bed. She made sure I was never alone for dinners and continues to cook meals for our family. She was the extra set of hands and eyes I had grown so accustomed to with Alex. My church family provided meals for the first six months. A group of women gave me diapers, wipes, household items, food, games for the kids, selfcare items, encouragement, and so much more every single month. The pastor at my church was the first one to come over the next morning after the accident. He is a resource I still use to this day.

We meet up every once in a while to catch up and talk about how things are going. Alex loved him and talking to him felt safe. All of these people made many sacrifices in their marriages and with their own families to be there for me and my kids when we needed them most.

Friends who lived close by made many efforts to keep me included in things going on. I didn't always want to leave the house, but getting the invitation always made me feel seen and cared for. They would come over for dinner so I wouldn't have to eat alone and play with the kids. They helped get the kids in their pajamas, fed Krew his evening bottle while I put Halle to bed, and helped clean up around the house.

My father in-law, usually a very stoic, unemotional person became someone I went to for many things. We would have long conversations together about the accident, autopsy, and questions we had. Every time he came over, he was trying to teach the kids something new. He wasn't a big fan of holding babies because it scared him (my dad is the same way), but he would ask to hold Krew. He helped babysit the kids during the week even though his wife was at work and not around to help him at times. Krew was his first diaper change. One day after Alex's dad, Paul, watched the kids, Krew came home with his diaper put on backwards. I had to laugh, but was grateful that he changed it! Paul had to take over doing all of the things for the house that Alex did. Hauling water, mowing the lawn, changing vents, spraying for bugs, etc. It is a task that he has taken on and we are forever grateful. We always knew that Paul loved us, but he has shown it now more than ever before.

Losing a loved one takes a tremendous toll on relationships. Decisions about belongings, the headstone, and money strained my relationship with my in-laws. My family's GoFundMe that was set up for support caused conflict with them, leading to lingering tension. Grief highlighted differences in how we coped. They were grieving their son and brother while I was grieving my husband and the father of my children. Our grief collided and it got messy. I felt ignored and undervalued, and struggled with feeling as though my young age was being used against me by Alex's family who were older and sometimes made me feel like my views didn't matter. The truth is, with death, one loses all control. We were all seeking ways to regain our sense of control over an uncontrollable situation. Despite the challenges, we continue to make an effort for the grandkids' sake, meeting weekly for dinner at Alex's parents house. While it hasn't always been easy, I am grateful for the progress we have made.

The amount of love, support, encouragement, help, and prayers we received was beyond incredible. Now I am able to look back on that time in my life and see just how quickly my village turned into a full fledged army for my family. People graciously provided meals, groceries, supplied diapers, wipes, pull-ups, snacks, toiletries, and all household needs. An overwhelming amount of donations were made. Our village cleaned my house, sent beautiful flowers, bought and donated clothes and shoes for the kids, blew up family pictures, sent gifts for the kids, framed song lyrics from Alex's funeral, and so much more.

Something I will never forget about that time in my life is the love and support that came from complete and total strangers from all around the world. People from all over reached out to tell me they heard my story and how it changed their lives. Strangers sent meaningful cards, anonymously donated breast milk for Krew, and, still to this day, continue to send me encouragement. I didn't know anything about these people, and they were willing to step up and help my family in our time of need. People who I knew in high school but were never really close with, sent encouraging letters with gifts for the kids and me.

The people I expected to be in my corner for that time in my life weren't necessarily there. People who I didn't know or ever expect to be a part of my inner circle showed up in ways I never expected. This was a hard truth to face at the moment. Now I realize that not everyone was supposed to be there for me. Not everyone can handle the severity and intensity that comes along with grief. It's uncomfortable and it's unknown territory. Whoever God places in your life to walk with you throughout your grief journey, is exactly who is meant to be there. You will find those messages of encouragement come through just when you need them the most. You will grow a special bond that knows no limits. You realize that death changes people, but it also changes you.

CHAPTER 12: AN IDENTITY AMPUTATED

"My grace is sufficient for you, for my power is made perfect in weakness. Therefore I will boast all the more gladly about my weaknesses, so that Christ's power may rest on me. That is why, for Christ's sake, I delight in weaknesses, in insults, in hardships, in persecutions, in difficulties. For when I am weak, then I am strong."
2 Corinthians 12:9-10 (NIV)

I met Alex when I was only nineteen years old. He showed me from the very first time we went out, that he was going to take care of me and provide for me– and he always did. Whenever I needed someone to talk to after a long day at work, he was there and listened. When I wasn't sure if I could make ends meet, he helped me. When I didn't know how to handle a situation, he guided me step by step. When I needed someone to just hold me and listen, he always did it so well. When I forgot ice at the store, he always willingly ran to grab it. When I wasn't feeling good, he was there to take care of Halle so I could stay in bed with soup and a binge-worthy show. Everything I knew about being a wife and a mother was because he was there with me. Together, we learned how to fulfill our roles and support each other in our tasks. It was a true partnership, and I didn't know how to do any of it without him. Alex and our children were the contributing factors as to how I understood myself. Now, I was alone without my support person, my safe place, and my biggest cheerleader. When I needed someone to hold me, no one compared to his hugs. When I needed someone to tell me the truth and give it to me straight, everyone was scared of how fragile I was. When I needed to just hear his voice, I couldn't. I was utterly lost. I had no idea who I was as a person without Alex. He was the other half of me that kept me going. With every day that passes without him, I feel myself turning into a better version of me that he will never get to see.

In his book, *A Grace Disguised*, Jerry Sittser so accurately compared catastrophic loss to undergoing an amputation of your identity. It is not like the literal amputation of a limb. Rather, it is more like the amputation of the self from the self. I only knew who I was because of the roles I played in my life, and now I felt like a stranger to myself and the world I was living in. My psyche is still programmed, even to this day, to look for Alex even when I know he is no longer here.

When the kids do something funny or hit a big milestone for the first time, I look for him to be there with me. When I have exciting news or something big happens, I pick up my phone to call him. After I put the kids to bed at night, I wait for him to crawl into bed and scratch my back. I am no longer a wife anymore, but I don't consider myself single. I am no longer one half of a parent team anymore, however much I wish I was. I am a widow and a solo parent. It is a confusing and heartbreaking identity to understand and navigate.

Who I was before June 10, 2021 passed the moment Alex did. That girl is gone. At first, I didn't know how to sleep anymore. I was constantly taking Tylenol to help ease the headaches from the crying. I was uncontrollably bleeding. I could physically feel my heart beating in my throat. My family was having to put food and water in front of me with gentle reminders that I need to eat and drink for Krew. My milk supply dropped drastically. I just felt numb every second of every day. I felt suffocated by my grief all the time.

A few months later, I realized the painful truth that I now had to figure out who I was without Alex. I had to decide who I wanted to be. I truly believe that death rearranges your life and your priorities. I wanted the best parts of Alex to live on in the kids and me. The way he embraced and accepted everybody, no matter who they were or what they believed. The way he listened and offered advice. The way he valued his love for us and would brag about us to anyone who would listen. Those were just a few of the things I wanted to make sure I kept doing for him.

My personality has changed. I went from being an organized, uptight, high maintenance, fun-loving, type A person to someone who is carefree, empathetic, flexible, and more type B. Recognizing my mortality made me start living my life more freely. The way I viewed my entire world had changed. Things I used to think were a substantial issue, no longer seemed so pressing. Things like making more money, remodeling our house, or wanting recognition at work no longer mattered to me. What mattered to me now was spending quality time with the people I love, having meaningful relationships with people, and figuring out my purpose in this life. I am more intentional now about how I live than ever before.

***

I started living my life constantly on high alert. My once safe world no longer felt safe. I just kept waiting for the next bad thing to happen. I saw the danger in every situation and was always thinking of the worst possible scenario. My anxiety loomed over me like a dark storm cloud.

Getting out of bed already took everything out of me, so leaving the house was equivalent to running a marathon at the time. I dreaded being around people and any social situation left me completely exhausted. The shallow conversations, the common struggles that I could no longer relate to and didn't have the patience to hear about, worrying if a trigger would arise and how I would handle it.

The pain of my loss both strengthened me as a whole and softened me to find more compassion for others who are suffering. I was forced to develop a new identity and with that came a new sense of independence, new interests, and a newfound love of things I never thought possible. I relied on Alex for everything since I met him. When we graduated college, I relied on him for a place to live. I relied on him to do all the financial work. I relied on him for all household and vehicle needs. I relied on him to be there for me whenever and wherever I needed him. Now that I didn't have him, I was determined to prove to myself that I could not only survive but thrive. I was twenty-six years old, but I never had that sense of independence before. I began fighting for things that really mattered to my kids and me. I never wanted to be perceived as difficult or make extra work for people, but I now realize that it's okay to fight for your needs without feeling like a burden. I am braver because of it.

It's no longer all about me, and I know that is such a self centered thing to say, but before the accident it was easy for me to slip into that habit. Without Alex, I realized how often I would make things about me and not even consider other people's feelings. I find myself being more intentional with other people and making sure to make every moment count since I never know when it will be my last. I have a new found desire to help other people feel supported and loved in their grief and hurt.

I have way more grace with others and myself. I allow myself to have a bad day and feel everything that I need to, but I don't dwell there. I joke about how this experience has aged me at least twenty years. I always considered myself to be an intelligent person, but this journey has made me wise. It's the kind of knowledge that comes only from experience and can't be taught in school.

***

I found myself constantly denying Alex's requests to get out of the house together for practical reasons. The kids were too young, we don't have a sitter, I'm still breastfeeding, I'm too tired, or even because I didn't feel like doing it. I feel so much regret because of that. I choose experiences now whenever I can. Take a last minute trip to go see a friend, attend a destination wedding, a weekend getaway, a football game, a concert, my answer will always be yes. Many of us have felt the weight of missed opportunities and the sting of regret. It's easy to get lost in the what-ifs and maybes, but it's important to remember that we have the power to create the life we want. Taking chances can often be the first step towards something great. You never know where they might lead you.

Death used to be a huge fear of mine. Eternity

freaked me out. Death no longer scares me. Not in a way that I want to take my own life, but in a way that I fully understand Jesus defeated the cross, and I get eternity with Him and Alex. Knowing that my eternity will be with Alex and he will be one of the first faces I see when I get there, makes me yearn for heaven in a way I never had before. It will be the most beautiful, joyous reunion.

I made a conscious effort to dig into my devotional and Bible to grow my relationship with God any chance I could get. Especially when I was all alone, and it was quiet in the house. I knew that if I didn't, the devil would seize the opportunity to speak self doubt and anxiety into my mind. I was the weakest and most vulnerable I had ever been in my entire life. Having faith in something much greater than me gave me the courage and hope I needed to persevere. I found that filling my mind with God's promises brought me a sense of comfort and peace, while sitting in the silence and letting my mind wander only intensified my doubt and anxiety. Through my readings and talking with God, I became closer to Him than I ever had been before. I had nothing tangible to hold onto for hope in my life. Everything as I knew it was crumbling around me and there was nothing I could do to stop it. I needed something I could cling to, and the only thing that gave me any sense of hope was God. So while I was in my valleys and at my lowest points, I would invite God to shift my perspective. To use this pain for His glory. To bring me supernatural peace. To help me walk by faith and not by sight. To surrender each and every part of my life and my heart. I came to Him exactly as I was, broken, confused, lonely, numb, whatever I was experiencing in that moment, and He met me there with open arms.

Steven Furtick, pastor of Elevation Church in North Carolina, said something during a sermon that has stuck with me. "Faith is believing in advance what will only make sense in reverse." It was so easy for me in those raw moments following the accident to wonder where God was. There was no way this was His plan. Looking back, I see God's hand in so many of the details that I never noticed before. The fact that Alex closed the blinds, sheltered me from seeing the accident. The song Waymaker playing on repeat in my head at the scene. Having Krew on my chest the entire time. Krew sleeping through the night for the first time the night before. It felt like God was giving me one last good night's rest before I wouldn't get another for a long time. Halle was able to go out to the farm with Alex earlier that night. Our last dinner together. Those final moments were full of love and bliss. My parents were in town just the week before to come meet Krew. That week Alex and my dad got the swing set put together for the kids. I kept reminding myself over and over again that even when it seems like God isn't working, He always is. I would remind myself that He is actively working things out for my good and His glory. Something more beautiful than I could even begin to imagine was in the works at that very moment. I just had to take a deep breath and trust. And that's exactly what I did.

When my worst nightmare became my reality, I found

an unexplainable and undeniable sense of peace that could only be found in God. It didn't make sense. I shouldn't have been experiencing peace about my situation, and yet, there I was feeling at peace with it because I knew God was with me. Whatever you're facing today that has you questioning if God is working in your life, please remember that you will one day be able to look back and see just how far He has carried you.

I saw a picture that described grief perfectly. It starts as a black circle. In the beginning of grief, this black circle is all you see and think about. You truly don't believe that it will ever go away. As time goes on, you begin to add memories and build around the black circle. You build new experiences, joy, love, purpose and other layers around it. That doesn't mean that you don't have moments of deep sorrow, and it doesn't mean the black circle gets any smaller or disappears. It just means, you can still build a life that is beautiful and meaningful to you while gaining strength to hold your grief and build your life around it.

CHAPTER 13: MY SECOND CHANCE AT LOVE

"He heals the brokenhearted, and binds up their wounds."
Psalm 147:3 (NIV)

Connor and Alex met the summer after high school in 2012. They were both from small towns and played against each other in sports but didn't really know each other. One summer night they ended up at the same party thanks to mutual friends. Connor's initial reaction to Alex was that he was weird. Alex just did and said whatever he wanted without thinking about the consequences sometimes. He did things his own way and on his own time. Later that summer, a group of guys went on a trip up to Wisconsin Dells. Connor and Alex got to know each other a little better on this trip, but they were still merely acquaintances.

Alex was heading to Kankakee Community College to play baseball. His plan was to take his general education classes there, and then transfer to Illinois State University to major in agriculture business for his remaining two years. Connor started at Illinois Wesleyan University to play football. After the football season, he transferred to Illinois State University so he could major in agriculture business. While Alex was attending KCC, he would come down to Bloomington almost every weekend to go out and usually stayed at Connor's place while he was there. Connor and Alex's friendship grew, but it wasn't until their junior year when Alex transferred to ISU and lived by Connor's condo that they became very close. They were with each other almost daily and if one of them was going out, the other was there with them.

On September 7, 2013, I was introduced to Connor for the first time. A group of us girls went to Lake Bloomington. My best friend at the time had an aunt who lived on the lake, and we would use her dock to swim and hangout. That friend also happened to be Connor's cousin. Connor came by with his boat and some of his friends to take us out. We hung out at the lake for a little while on the boat and then decided that we would head to Connor's condo for a pregame that night. That is where I met Alex for the first time. He was wearing a gray American Eagle t-shirt and Buckle jeans. I was wearing a mint green tank top with American Eagle jeans. No one introduced Alex to me, he caught my eye all on his own. The first thing I ever said to him was, "You smell good!" and the rest was history.

During college and even a few years after, Alex helped Connor's family farm operation during harvest by running the grain cart for them. Alex loved doing this. He said that Connor and him were constantly just talking back and forth on the walkie talkies. Alex adored Connor's whole family. He joked with me at times telling me about how Connor's mom told him that if he weren't with me, she would want him with one of her daughters.

Four years later, in March of 2017, Alex proposed to me. I asked him if he had told his friends ahead of time. Of course he called Connor and the other three guys who were living in that house at the time to tell them that he was going to ask me to marry him. At the time, we were the only people in our friend group who were engaged, so they all teased him about it but ultimately knew he was ready for it. We got married in June of 2018, and it was very hard for Alex to pick groomsmen because he had so many friends, but Connor made the cut without question.

Whenever Alex and I would go out, Connor was usually there. Connor was someone Alex would call on a regular basis and vice versa. If you haven't gathered by now, Alex loved talking, but he was also a really good listener and advice giver. One of the many things Connor loved most about him, too.

In the months following the accident, Alex's friends were kind enough to check-in on me. They would stop by with dinner, send check-in texts, and play with the kids whenever they got the chance. Especially his friends who were now in relationships or married.

On Alex's birthday, October 10, 2021, I invited a bunch of family and friends over to honor him. We released balloons, put floating lanterns in the pond, and sent lanterns up in the sky. All of us gathered around down by the pond in our backyard and prayed together. Then we sang happy birthday and ate the same Dairy Queen ice cream cake I got for him every year. A bunch of us sat out on the deck that night telling stories about Alex and crying together. Connor is a farmer, so the beginning of October is a busy part of the year with harvest. I remember being surprised that he even made it out for Alex's birthday.

The next day when I got the mail, I found a letter inside from Connor. In the letter he reminisced about Alex's birthdays in the past and some of the things they did to celebrate together. He talked about how many times he's wanted to pick up the phone to call and talk with Alex. Then, he apologized for not checking in and reaching out to me more. He had lost one of his best friends and his girlfriend of four years (not a death, but a break up) within a month of each other. He mentioned that he stayed updated by reading my posts on social media and those helped motivate him to keep going. He ended his letter with, "Keep battling Kell, we're all rooting for you."

I read the letter multiple times, the same way I did with every letter I got at the time, and just cried. I texted him to say thank you for the letter and that it meant a lot to me. From there, more check-in texts were sent, and we found we were talking to each other throughout the days until we would go to bed.

I was still getting a lot of meals from so many people, and I needed help eating all the food. I remember getting a big lasagna one night, and I immediately texted a bunch of friends to come over and help me eat it all. Six friends came over that night, and one of them was Connor. He had just gotten a new dog, Ava, who came along too. Everyone had just come from work and was wearing sweatpants and a t-shirt of some sort. Connor was the only one wearing jeans. We all made fun of him for this. It was such a good night. I hated eating alone and loved that my home was filled with people and dogs— like it always used to be.

Connor and I began snapchatting each other more. He would send pictures of Ava, and I would send pictures or videos of the kids just being themselves. The check-in texts started to become more and more frequent, but they were different than they were with anyone else. It didn't seem like a chore for him to do it. It didn't feel superficial. It was also a way for me to see how things were going with him since I knew he wasn't processing his grief with his friends.

Six months after Alex passed, someone watched the kids for me, and I drank for my first time since getting pregnant with Krew. Following the accident, I was terrified to drink because my emotions were so delicate and unpredictable. I wasn't sure how alcohol would affect me in my fragile state. When I finally decided to have a drink, I wanted to be surrounded by friends in a place where I felt safe. Some of us met up at a friend's house and then headed to a small town bar. We didn't stay very long, and some friends took me home and stayed to talk with me for a while. On the way home, I was already thinking about how I was going to be alone for the first time. No kids, no monitors to watch, no baby sleeping in the room with me, I would be completely alone in a quiet house and that terrified me. I texted Connor and asked if he would come over for a little bit so I wouldn't have to be alone. He came over that night wearing boots, jeans, and a dark gray long sleeve waffle-knit shirt. I had changed into sweats and a sweatshirt when I got home from the bar. We sat on the living room floor and just talked. I told him about how confusing everything was and how helpless I felt all the time. I cried on him, and eventually I fell asleep with my head on his shoulder. At that point, he told me I should probably go to sleep, and he should probably get home to do the same. He had to wake up early to drive to a Packers game the next morning.

From that day on, we talked everyday. I noticed myself starting to get excited when his name popped up on my phone. I found myself smiling more throughout the day. It was the week before Christmas break at work and during our Christmas party in class, I was playing Christmas music and dancing with my students. I remember stopping in that moment and actually feeling a sense of joy for the first time without feeling guilty. Connor came over two times that week before I left for Florida over Christmas break. I would wait until the kids were sleeping and then he would come over for a few hours and then head home. We would just sit on the couch in the living room, watch *All American* on Netflix, and catch up with each other.

I had done a lot of work on myself in order to feel like I was ready to be in a relationship, but I wanted to be sure I was making the right decision not only for myself but for my kids. Before I let myself fall for him, or even begin a relationship, I prayed fervently and asked God for specific signs that Connor was a part of His plan. I asked for the door to be slammed shut if it wasn't His plan, so that I could be sure. I prayed for very specific signs, such as handwritten notes, as I have always had a soft spot for them. Before I left for Florida that Christmas break, in my mailbox I found a present with red and black buffalo plaid wrapping paper. Inside the present was the book, *Lemons on Friday*, with a card and letter from Connor. *Lemons on Friday* was written by Mattie Jackson Smith who is the daughter of the famous country singer, Alan Jackson. Connor is a huge country music fan. The song *Racing the Dark* by Alan Jackson started playing one day on his Pandora station. He found it catchy at first, but then started catching on to the storyline. He thought there was a deeper meaning behind the song so he looked into it. Turns out the song was co-written by his daughter, Mattie who unexpectedly lost her husband at twenty-eight years old. He looked into Mattie even further and found out that she wrote a whole book on coping with tragic loss called *Lemons on Friday*. He bought the book, read it first to make sure it would be something I would like, wrote me a letter, looked up on YouTube how to wrap said book, and left it in my mailbox. When I found it and realized all of this, I began to fall for Connor.

You may recall in the first chapter that the night Alex died, he dropped seed off to a friend… and he was the last friend to ever see him before he left this earth. Now you've met him. His name is Connor.

Connor (L) & Alex (R) at our wedding 2018

CHAPTER 14: MOVING FORWARD, NOT MOVING ON

"In their hearts humans plan their course, but the Lord establishes their steps."
Proverbs 16:9 (NIV)

Just days after the accident we were picking out Alex's gravesite at the cemetery. A comment was made about getting me a plot next to Alex. My father-in-law said something to the extent that he hopes I get remarried. I burst into even more tears. My mother-in-law, also crying, gave me a hug and said, "I hope so, too. I don't want you to be alone forever." I hugged her back and said, "No, I have the kids. They will keep me busy." Just days after losing my husband, I had no intention of ever remarrying again because I was fully aware of the heart breaking cost.

My experience is all I can offer to share with you. It's important to remember that there is no rulebook on widowhood, no set timeline for beginning to date again, and no formula to decipher it all. This is a delicate subject, and I want to approach it with the utmost sensitivity.

After months of paralyzing loneliness and deafening silence, I began to do extensive work on myself that I knew needed to be done. I did personal development, devotional readings, read my Bible, and prayed continuously throughout the day everyday. Through my tears, I would tell God I didn't want to be alone forever, as if He didn't already know. I didn't pray to God as if He were a genie who grants wishes, I was simply telling Him my desires that almost seemed like a secret at the time. Being a wife and mom just made sense to me; it felt like what I was put on this earth to do and I believed it was my calling. With that, I also told Him that I was fully surrendering my life to Him. I laid down my life hour after hour, minute after minute, until I fully believed it. I found peace in telling God that if He was calling me to be a widow for the rest of my life, then so be it. If that was His greater plan for me, I knew that would give me more joy and purpose than anything else. And I fully believed this.

The best way I can describe dating after losing your spouse is comparing it to having your second child. I remember crying to Alex near the end of my pregnancy with Krew because I was so nervous about entering this completely uncharted territory and having to split my love and time between both of my babies. Halle had never had to share us before. The three of us were all we ever knew. I was worried about what our new family dynamic would be like and how I could possibly love our next child as much as I loved Halle. The second Krew was born, my heart instantly expanded. I didn't diminish my love for even a second; I doubled it. That's exactly how it is with dating after death. I will always love Alex. My love for him will never leave me or change. But with Connor, my heart, also, instantly expanded. I am able to hold room for both Alex and Connor in my heart in the same way I am able to hold love for both Halle and Krew. I didn't realize this until I was in it. It is a beautiful process if you let your heart expand in ways you never knew you could before.

When Connor came into the picture, I prayed for signs and discernment to see things clearly. My kids always come first so I wanted to make sure my emotions weren't getting the better of me and clouding my judgment. The more time I spent getting to really know Connor, the more I found that things were effortlessly falling into place. It became very clear to me that Connor was not only a part of God's plan, but the answer to all my silent prayers.

Finding someone who loves a widow is no small feat. I truly believe that God was preparing Connor specifically for the kids and me. I remember being so scared to tell Alex's friends that Connor and I were seeing each other. Two friends in particular scared me the most, Andrew and Tanner, Alex's best friends. Andrew and his wife live in North Carolina so I Facetimed to tell them about Connor and me. I'll never forget immediately after finding out Andrew looked at me and said, "Kellie this is the best case scenario. I don't think Alex would have ever admitted it, but if he had to pick someone for you and the kids, it would be Connor." I instantly felt lighter. Andrew and Alex had the same brain, so hearing him say that, reassured me that this was a good choice. Then, I had Tanner and his girlfriend come over for dinner one night so I could tell them about Connor and me. They claimed they already knew about us, but were excited for us nonetheless. Telling both of them felt like a God wink to encourage me.

Connor and I had many extensive and elaborate conversations about what it would look like to date before we were even official. I didn't have time for something that was just going to be "for fun." I didn't want to take any of my already insignificant energy away from the kids. I repeatedly drilled him with questions for hours… I would come up with something in the middle of the night and call him to see how he would respond to whatever type of situation came up in my mind. *What if I wanted to be done having kids? What if I can't have any more kids? What if the kids call you dad? What if the kids ask you about Alex? How would you handle disciplining the kids? Will you come to church with me?* You name it, I asked him. I made it very clear from the very beginning that my kids come first no matter what, and that Alex would always be a part of our lives. I want my kids to know their dad and I reminded him that my love for Alex was never going to go away. His response was, "I wouldn't have it any other way."

Dating a widow is a heck of a lot more complicated than traditional dating. I am certain that God prepares special people to be with a widow/widower. It is not by chance. He has to be secure in himself, but humble enough to know that she will forever love someone else. He has to embrace her heart with the most gentle touch, knowing it is still carefully being pieced back together. He has to acknowledge her strength while protecting her vulnerability. He has to see her for who she is without allowing her loss to define her. It is a significant undertaking that cannot be handled by just anyone.

One of the hardest parts about dating after death is all the guilt that comes with it. It swallows you whole... the feeling of cheating on your late husband – it's brutal. You are fighting yourself constantly on every little decision and how it will affect your kids. Ironically enough, Alex and I had a conversation one night about what we would want the other one to do if something were to happen to us. I told him I would still want him to be happy and remarry. He always brushed these comments off saying, "Kellie, that's not going to happen. I have to be the one to go first because I can't live without you." One night I finally pushed and made him give me an answer, which I'm so thankful that I did. He told me he would want me to be happy and remarry, too. He would want me to live the rest of my days on

Earth to the fullest. I remind myself of this conversation often as it helps lift the burden of guilt immensely. I also think about our kids. Alex was the best daddy to our babies, and they got so little time with him. While no one can ever replace him, I am certain that he would want a good father figure in our kids' lives to do everything with them that he never got the chance to do. Although the guilt eventually fades, it never fully disappears. It's not an all-consuming feeling, and it rarely affects me when it comes to dating anymore. As long as you're doing it with the best of intentions, when you're ready, and for the right reasons, you deserve to be happy.

One of the scariest parts of dating after death is confronting your in-laws about a new man and bringing him into your children's lives. I wasn't sure how they would take hearing the news, especially since our relationship changed so drastically after the accident. It was exactly nine months since Alex passed when I invited my in-laws over for dinner. After eating, we went into the living room where the kids played around us. They sat on the couch while I sat alone on the floor wearing my black leggings and olive green sweater. My anxiety was palpable — my palms were sweating, my face turning red, and my legs were shaking visibly. Despite my fears, I took a deep breath and began to speak. I explained that Connor would never replace Alex, that Alex would always be the kids' dad, and that it was crucial for us to keep his memory alive for the children. I was sweating, shaking, and crying, but I knew how important it was to have this conversation. Most importantly, I assured them that this wouldn't change their relationship with their grandkids. When I told them it was Connor, they both said, "Oh, I like him. He's a good guy." It was important to me that they hear about our relationship from me and not through the grapevine. I wanted to reassure them that I could never and will never forget about Alex. My mother-in-law shed a few tears, but they were both happy for me. Now, nineteen months after initially breaking the news to them, they have embraced Connor and invite him to holidays and weekly dinners. My brother-in-law and his wife have also embraced Connor and make him feel included during their kids' birthday parties or holiday get-togethers. I can only imagine that this is not easy for them to see or maybe even sometimes understand, but their acceptance means a lot to me, and I know it does to Connor as well.

***

People can be so quick to judge and tell you that you "moved on" too quickly and, while I know it shouldn't, their judgment stings. It makes you question everything all over again. Something that my grief has taught me is to have grace for the people who don't understand. It used to be me. I just as easily could've thought, from the outside looking in, that someone starting to talk to a different person six months after losing their husband was "too soon." Because six months to a person who isn't grieving and living in survival mode, is completely different than six months for someone who is. I had to learn how to have grace for these people who had never encountered the magnitude of grief as I knew it because one day, they might, and their minds will probably change. But it's not my job to change their minds. I just want to raise awareness that grief knows no timeline, and we should avoid attempting to impose one on those affected by it.

Since Alex was the only person I ever dated and we married young, I had no idea what dating was like for people my age – let alone with kids. I was adamant that I didn't want Connor being around the kids until I really knew for sure that he was going to stick around. After almost two months of him coming over late at night after the kids went to bed, and then driving home late at night to get to sleep, I finally let him around the kids. Halle was two and a half and Krew was 10 months old at the time. Valentine's Day that year, 2022, was the first time the four of us had dinner all together. He brought over steaks and twice baked potatoes to make for dinner. Halle, Connor, and I sat at the small wooden table in the living room and Krew was in his high chair next to us. My kids were used to having visitors over for dinner, so that night it was just a different person who they had seen before but only briefly. Connor was nervous and even awkward at times with the kids. He had been around kids but wasn't super comfortable with them. He had never changed a diaper, fed a baby a bottle, or given a child a bath. If he was holding a baby and they started crying, he automatically handed them back to their parents as one does when they aren't familiar with the shushing, bouncing technique that comes so naturally to parents. As he spent more time with the kids, he gained confidence and insight that came seamlessly. He quickly built connections with them on a deeper level and spent the time getting to know their individual needs and unique personalities. He became the kids' go to guy for playing and I loved watching them together laughing until it hurt. Chasing them around in the living room, jumping on the trampoline, playing hide and seek, you name it, he did it effortlessly. It has been such a privilege to watch him go from uncomfortable with all kids in general, to establishing a confident, loving, and trustworthy relationship with my kids.

I am a very open person and wear all my feelings on my sleeve. Connor, on the other hand, is the complete opposite. He doesn't like talking about his feelings; he just needs time to process things and then he can move on. So when I'm having a bad day, or week, due to grief, it is important that Connor asks how I need to be comforted in that moment because it changes. Sometimes I want to be alone and process it, sometimes I just want him to hold me and not ask questions, sometimes I want his opinion on it, and sometimes I want him to just listen. Let me be clear that dating does not fix my grief. It isn't magically gone because I have a boyfriend. The grief is always there; I am just learning how to move forward with it. I still have my bad days and when they happen, Connor does his best to do what I need in that moment or try to make me laugh.

Ultimately, it comes down to communication. In order for me not to take it out on him when I'm having a bad day or week, I need to tell him what I need, and he tries his best to deliver. I've also had to keep in mind that Connor is also grieving a friend, so empathy and understanding are crucial. Being transparent and maintaining an open line of communication is key during times of sorrow.

People ask me all the time how Connor feels about me talking and posting about Alex on social media. They ask if it makes him feel like he's living in Alex's shadow or constantly feeling like number two. When I said God prepares a special kind of man to be with a widow, I meant it. He knew and loved Alex, too and that is so comforting to me that I never have to explain to him who he was to me. He wants to honor Alex just as much as I do. Connor understands that I have a very vulnerable personality, and writing or talking about it helps me. I don't do it to cause hurt or jealousy to Connor, I do it to help myself cope with the grief and keep him alive the only way I can now. Even though we are both painfully aware that the only reason we are together is because Alex is not here, it doesn't define our relationship. Our relationship is completely different because I am completely different. Connor isn't my second choice, he's my second chance that I'm honestly not even sure I deserve at times.

I didn't ask for this to happen. I didn't want to be in this situation. I didn't have a choice. I am learning how to find the joy in life again, and Connor has truly helped bring me back to life. The hole in my heart for Alex will never be filled, and Connor will never replace him. They are two completely different relationships and people. I know, first hand, what it's like to lose the person I vowed to spend the rest of my life with. If, and when, I allow myself to open up my heart again, knowing the paralyzing cost, it is brave. True love is standing in the midst of what you've gone through and continuing to love people rather than letting your heart get calloused for fear that you'll get hurt again.

There's a quote by Anne Gettes that says, "Any man can be a father, but it takes someone special to be a dad." I think about this all the time. I cannot tell you why God picked Alex to be Halle and Krew's father while simultaneously choosing Connor to be their dad in this life. Perhaps it's because being a father is a biological distinction, while being a dad is a title that must be earned through love, dedication, and sacrifice. Alex still holds both of those titles, but everyday I watch Connor work hard to be the kind of dad that the kids deserve. He shows up to events, helps with discipline, teaches them right from wrong, and leads by example. This is not the life I envisioned for myself, but there is beauty amidst the brokenness.

CHAPTER 15: THE LIGHT

"He will swallow up death forever. The Sovereign Lord will wipe away the tears from all faces."
Isaiah 25:8 (NIV)

Megan Devine, a psychotherapist, writer, and grief advocate, said, "We've got this idea that there are only two options in grief: you're either broken and unable to function or you're healed and 'over it.' Nothing else in life is black and white like that, so why do we treat grief as though it has an on-off switch?" I thought this was such a perfect example of living with both grief and joy because I, too, used to believe this point of view. I thought that it was impossible to experience grief and joy simultaneously. I am now grateful for the opportunity to change my perspective and acknowledge that living with both emotions is possible. It's not all or nothing.

Some days are good, some days are just okay, and other days are unbearable. The grief is forever a part of me, and I haven't forgotten for a single second since 9:13 pm on June 10, 2021 what happened to my family.

In the early days and months, all I could see was the pain and devastating hurt; there was no joy to be found. I would find myself getting angry when people would tell me that it would get better in time because I just didn't see how that was possible. All I saw was pitch black darkness everywhere I looked. But the good news is that the darkness never wins because the light always overcomes.

Imagine you're in a room with no windows, no lights, and the door is closed. It is completely black and you cannot see anything. Then, imagine that someone turns on a flashlight. Where is the first place you look? To the flashlight. It will take your eyes a second to adjust after being in the darkness, but once you do, the light is all you see and you use it to help you get out. That's exactly what God does for us. Jesus says, *I am the light of the world. Whoever follows me will never walk in darkness, but will have the light of life.* John 8:12 *(NIV)* What a beautiful and humbling reminder that even when we think we're alone, Jesus is right there with us. He lived on earth as a human just like us. He felt all the emotions that we feel. He understands what grief and hurt and pain feel like. He knows how it feels to weep. He understands that we live in a broken world filled with sorrow and hurt.

I've learned that there is a difference between happiness and joy. Happiness is a feeling based on temporary circumstances. For example, you get into the college you wanted. You go to a concert with your friends. You eat your favorite chocolate. Happiness is surface level and a feeling that we can obtain from many earthly things. It comes and goes depending on our circumstances. But joy isn't contingent on any circumstance and is found within. A lot of times, joy defies your circumstances. For in the heart of Jesus, we discover the essence of true joy, a joy that transcends all earthly boundaries and endures eternally.

It took me a few months, but through the grace of God, I have found joy in many areas of my life. Nothing about my circumstances made me happy in any sort of way, but seeing how God provided for my family, the people He brought into our lives, and the deep relationship I gained with Him gave me a sense of joy. I remember having an overwhelming feeling of peace about my life and moving forward. I went from being scared to death about raising two kids by myself, providing for them, and relearning how to function in my everyday life again… to being at peace. It didn't make any sense. I shouldn't have felt at peace about any part of my situation, but I did. I knew exactly where my strength continued to come from to get me through each and everyday, and it was so humbling to know that it wasn't from me.

Sometimes we feel like holding on to our grief makes us closer to the person that we lost, which makes our grief become sacred to us. We feel like holding on to it helps us stay closer to our lost loved one in some way.

But I assure you, even if you wanted to, you could never forget them. These moments of wanting to hold tight to our grief can sneak up on us at random times throughout the day. But living your life to find the joy in your day to day life means you're living with hope. Earth is not our forever home, Heaven is. God has each of us here for a reason, and it's up to us to trust that He kept us here for a purpose.

In the beginning, the pain can be so raw and all consuming that all we see is the darkness and the hurt. But slowly and through hope, we smile, and then we laugh, and then we love. Our hearts are no doubt still shattered, nothing we ever do or say could ever change our devastating loss. But when your baby gives you a big, slobbery, open mouthed kiss for the first time. When your toddler sees you at pick up and runs to you full force with open arms to give you the biggest hug. When your kids are belly laughing together. When you find these moments of joy, you are - slowly but surely - being carefully pieced back together and relearning what can bring you joy in your life.

For me, milestones, big events, and all my children's firsts, are some of the most bittersweet moments. You are filled with so much joy that you and your children are thriving despite all odds, and you are so proud of how far all of you have come together. But on the other hand, these moments are also when your heart aches the most because your person isn't here to witness all the joy with you. It's just another painful reminder that they are no longer here. Two opposing emotions can live together, you don't have to choose between finding joy in your life or living in a constant state of grief. They are both going to come, and sometimes both emotions can live in perfect harmony, other times they are completely out of balance, knocking your life out of rhythm.

One of the biggest things that helped me was looking at other widows' stories and finding hope through them. Through social media, I connected with many other widows and I had no idea that so many of us were so young— it was heartbreaking and hopeful all at once. I was watching women who were a few years ahead in the widowhood journey, getting remarried, having more kids, blending families, giving praise to God, and living a life filled with joy and hope and also grief. It helped me see that I was not alone in my journey and anything is possible with God.

There is no pause button in life. It keeps moving whether we're ready for it or not. I don't want to miss all the unbelievably joyous moments that come even in the simple, mundane everyday tasks. There are no words, prayers, or wishes I could say to ever make my grief go away. It will always be a part of who I am. I am thankful for it in some ways. It has taught me so much about who I am, how capable I am, and how God desires a closer relationship with me. When the sadness comes and washes over me, I let it. I feel it all deeply. I experience these emotions differently at times. Sometimes that means looking at a picture, going right back to that setting, remembering it all and a big smile comes to my face. Other times, that means sitting on the bathroom floor, gasping for air, and feeling numb to this reality that I am still adjusting to. But I also never want to miss the joy that is also so present in my day to day life. When someone makes dinner for my family. When Halle sings a song at the loudest volume possible. When Krew practices sports and makes a deep grunting noise. Hearing their laughter while I chase them around the couch in the living room. Getting a handwritten card in the mail. I don't want to miss out on those moments either. It's a difficult balance to understand, but once you acknowledge that God meant for these emotions to coexist, and how desperately we need them both in our lives, it changes everything.

CHAPTER 16: EVERYTHING *DOESN'T* HAPPEN FOR A REASON

"My command is this: Love each other as I have loved you."
John 15:12 (NIV)

I never knew what to say to someone going through a tragic loss before my own. I always wanted to say something to acknowledge their hurt, but the only things I could ever think to say were all of the cliche sayings. *Let me know if you need anything. God gives his toughest battles to his strongest soldiers. Everything happens for a reason.* Those were the things that came to my mind as I didn't know any better. Now that I've been on the other side, I've learned a lot about what is helpful and what is hurtful.

In my experience, everyone who has said these cliche

sayings or acknowledges loss in any sort of way is always coming from a good place. I appreciate people making an effort over saying nothing. The reality is that there is nothing you can say to a grieving person that will make them feel better or change their circumstances. When you tell someone who has just experienced a loss that everything happens for a reason, it invalidates their feelings and diminishes the loss. It's okay to simply say, "I am so sorry. I have no words."

Jesus never intended for our world to be broken and painful. Sometimes, we will never understand the reason behind why things happen or why people are taken too soon from us. It really is just as bad as we think. Starting a sentence with "at least" can be hurtful and unproductive. Although people may use it to express empathy, it can be difficult to hear in times of distress. For example, hearing "at least you have kids" or "at least you have a boy and a girl" can be upsetting. Of course, I am grateful for my children, but it doesn't make the painful experience any less traumatic.

Grieving people don't need to be told how strong they are. We are surviving and forced to be strong. In the initial days and weeks after my husband died, I'd never felt more weak — and it didn't just last a day or two. I had children to take care of and a job to do. I couldn't let myself fall apart. The one person I leaned on the most for my strength and confidence was no longer here. I had to relearn how to do everything on my own. I knew I wouldn't be labeled as strong if Alex was still here, so that made me angry being reminded of it.

Grieving people don't need advice, opinions, judgments or solutions. It can be frustrating when individuals try to relate to your experience when they haven't gone through the same thing. Avoid comparing losses or suggesting solutions such as exercise or telling someone it will get better with time. These comments can unintentionally invalidate the person's feelings. It's best to simply listen and offer your support without trying to "fix" things.

One of the most common phrases people said to me was, "If there's anything you need, please let me know." While they had good intentions, it meant absolutely nothing to me at the time. *I can't let you know what I need when I don't even know what I need myself!* I was in survival mode and only thinking about things that were absolutely necessary to make it through the next second. Their offer felt more like empty, meaningless words to me. It would have been better to have been asked very specific questions. This helps a grieving person feel comfortable to accept the help they need without feeling like a burden. It shows that you're thinking about them and how best to serve them in a time when they can't think for themselves. Examples of this would be: "I am going to bring you dinner this week. Which day works best for you?" Or "I am taking the kids to the park, would you like me to keep them overnight or bring them back?" Or "I hired a cleaning service for your house so you don't have to worry about that. What is the best day next week for them to come?" Or "I am going to come over. While I'm there, do you prefer I do laundry, cook, or take care of the kids? I'm doing one of those." These were some of the most helpful things people did for me that allowed me to receive the help I desperately needed but didn't know how to ask for.

Checking in with a grieving person is so important. Not just for the first few days and weeks, but years after. There is no right or wrong way to go about this. Whenever you feel inclined, always reach out and tell them you're thinking about them, or they're doing a great job, or their person is so proud of them. Maybe you're in the car and a song comes on the radio that reminds you of them or a memory with them. Maybe you see someone who looks just like them. Maybe you had a dream with them in it. Those texts of people remembering Alex always come to me at the most perfect times when I need them the most. You are helping to honor our loved one and us as we move forward. We need to feel seen. I always tell people to remember the big dates. Those include, the date of the month they passed away on, their birthday, wedding anniversary, and of course the actual date they passed away. Other days that don't need to be remembered but definitely acknowledged would be any holidays, kids' birthdays, and big milestone events in their lives. Sometimes when you send a message to check in, you won't get a response. Please don't take that personally. Sometimes we are just so emotionally and mentally drained from the day, or having a bad day, or the message stirs up something in us that we didn't even know was there. I promise that we see and appreciate your messages, so please don't stop sending them. We will regain our capacity to interact again one day. Checking in goes a long way and those experiencing the grief will always remember the people who did this for them.

If you are a part of the grieving person's inner circle, please show up physically for them. They are not going to want to go anywhere or do anything, but they need you to show up for them even if it feels like they're pushing you away. Go to them. Say their person's name. Ask questions. Most importantly, be willing to sit in the silence with them. I know that may be uncomfortable, but sometimes just having someone sit in the silence lets us know that we're not alone, we're loved, and we're seen. Your presence does more than you know.

My kids were so small at the time that I needed the most help with them. I needed help feeding, dressing, playing, transporting, and loving them. I was never alone and constantly being needed by one or both of them 24/7. When someone would take the kids, even for a half hour, it felt like I really got the chance to breathe and let it all out instead of having it hold it all in for them.

The other area I needed the most help with was my house. I did the best I could, but my house was falling apart and becoming a mess. My mother in-law asked me one night, "Kellie, don't take this the wrong way, but can I get you someone to clean the house?" I took no offense to that comment because it was obvious that my chores had been put on the back burner while we were surviving. Coming home from work to a clean house that smelled fresh was such a relief. I did text the cleaning ladies and ask them not to touch any of Alex's things that were out. I had them right where he left them and I wasn't ready to move them yet.

If you are at their house and want to help with laundry, dishes, or basic cleaning tasks, please make sure you ask if there's anything they do not want you to touch or move. My family stayed with me at my house for the first few days and weeks that followed. They all just wanted to help, and I didn't know what to ask them to help with. So they started helping around the house. Alex's clear Coca-Cola cup that he left on top of the Culligan water jug in the kitchen got put in the dishwasher and cleaned. Alex's big dark gray body towel that was hanging up over the side of the shower got used and washed. Alex's last pile of laundry in the laundry room got washed. The clothes Alex was wearing that night in the accident got washed before I even saw them. Those were some of the very last scents and pieces of Alex that I had left in our house. Those things can never be undone. No one did these things maliciously with the intention of hurting me, but they didn't know to ask. Please ask first before using or touching anything. To an outsider, it may seem like something small and maybe doesn't even make sense to you, but I promise there is a reason they haven't touched it in weeks, months, or even years. Although I wanted to cling to the remaining pieces of Alex, I recognize that others may not share my sentiments, and that is perfectly acceptable. Just remember to be considerate of their feelings – if they don't want something touched, there's often a more profound reasoning that may not be apparent to you.

CHAPTER 17: REDEMPTION

"I consider that our present sufferings are not worth comparing with the glory that will be revealed in us."
Romans 8:18 (NIV)

I once heard that we can't always control our reaction, but we can control our response. My initial reaction after losing Alex was that I didn't want to be here without him. I didn't want to get out of bed in the morning. I didn't want to go to work. I didn't want to do anything. I was so miserable in this new world without him. But I had two little kids who depended on me for every single thing. I didn't mean to keep waking up and going through the motions— it just happened. The more time I had to process my loss, I realized that while I didn't want to be here without Alex, God kept me here for a reason.

He's not done with me yet. So while I'm still living, I decided to take control of how I spent the rest of my fleeting days here.

I was immediately reminded of two powerful stories of redemption in the Bible: Job and Ruth. Job is perhaps the most well-known story about suffering and pain, along with God's care, protection, and ultimate blessing. In short, Job was a blameless and upright man who had 7 sons, 3 daughters, 7,000 sheep, 3,000 camels, 500 oxen, 500 donkeys, and a large number of servants. He was the greatest man among all the people in the East (Job 1:1-2). Satan believed that Job was only righteous because God had favored him generously. In one day, Job loses his ten children, all his livestock, and all servants to invaders and natural disasters. Job still praised God. Job is then afflicted with horribly painful skin sores. Job's wife and friends all tried to get him to turn against God, but he never did. Job continued to trust God through his pain. In the end, God blessed Job with 14,000 sheep, 6,000 camels, 1,000 oxen, 1,000 donkeys, 7 sons, and 3 daughters (Job 42:12). God returned to Job what was stolen and doubled everything, besides his children. The moral of the story? God promises to restore that which was lost and return to us that which was stolen.

The story of Ruth sticks out to me a little bit more for a few reasons. Ruth was widowed young, Ruth is my niece's name, and my pastor talked about Ruth during Alex's funeral. The story of Ruth provides a glimpse of hope and redemption that can come even in the midst of overwhelming chaos and suffering. Ruth lived in Moab and was married to Mahlon, who was one of Naomi and Elimelek's sons. First, Naomi loses her husband, and ten years later, she loses both of her sons. Naomi tells both of her daughter in-laws that she is going back to Judah. Orpah, Naomi's other daughter in-law, stays in Moab with her family. Ruth however clings to Naomi and says, "Where you go I will go, and where you stay I will stay. Your people will be my people and your God my God." (Ruth 1:16 - NIV). Ruth, who knew nothing about God, was determined to stay by Naomi's side and chose to cling to God, forsaking all that she had ever known to follow Him. In the end, God provided for both Naomi and Ruth and restored their emptiness and bitterness. Ruth goes on to marry a man named Boaz, and gives birth to a son, Obed. The story of Ruth shows how God preserves his people, restores dignity, and gives hope for the future. That was exactly what I needed at the time.

***

Early the next morning after the accident, I was sitting on the couch in my living room, in the same spot I always sit, talking with my pastors. I remember them asking me what they needed the church to do for me. Without hesitation, I told them, "I need people to pray for me to remember God's promises." I was wearing Alex's red Kankakee baseball t-shirt and his gray Nike sweatpants. My face and eyes were swollen from crying so much. The bags under my eyes were turning black from no sleep in over 36 hours. I remember my sister trying to get the kids dressed to take them outside so I could talk with my pastors, but Krew was being fussy and just wanted me. The only thing I could think of that I was positive I needed immediately after losing Alex was Jesus. I knew that if there was any chance of me surviving this, I needed a redemption story. In my heart I knew God's promises, but my head seemed to be working against me because nothing made sense to me then.

God's word became like a handle for me to hold on to during turbulence, and it slowly started to give me glimpses of hope for the future. I'll never forget, during Alex's funeral, my pastor talked a lot about the power of *yet*.

"I am empty and devastated and yet, He will be faithful. Yet, He knows what I don't know. Yet, as sad, mad, angry, and confused as I am, He is still good. Yet, I am not abandoned. Yet, He is a father to the fatherless. Yet, He is my redeemer who brings beauty from ashes."

I clung to those statements and prayed every single day that the power of them would be worked in my life. Even in the darkest part of my life, God was still working out a plan of redemption. When I would remind myself of His promises, it reinforced the truth in my own heart and mind. As soon as I made the decision to do this, I felt something powerful and awakening in my soul.

I've always been the type of person who likes to write out my feelings. It helped me acknowledge where I was at and discern what God says in the Bible about my feelings to encourage me. I used to keep diaries when I was younger, then when I got older, I would write out notes on my phone. I was always afraid to share my writing because it is so vulnerable. After the accident, however, it became therapeutic for me to process through writing and then share it with the world as captions of posts on social media. When I started, it was simply a way for me to express my feelings, but it quickly became so much bigger than that. I had no idea how many people would resonate with my raw emotions. I found a community of grieving people who I had never met in real life thanking me for putting words to feelings they have never been able to articulate. I started to realize that the more vulnerable and raw I became about sharing my story and my grief, I was no longer just helping myself, but others, too.

During Alex's wake, I'll never forget a colleague giving me a hug and saying in my ear, "Because of you, I'm starting to believe in God." People were dumbfounded that in my crisis I was turning to God instead of turning my back on Him. They didn't understand, and they began to ask questions. At first, I felt like a fraud because I am no expert and certainly not a model Christian. I am a flawed human who falls short every day in many ways. But then I realized, that's exactly who God uses. Regular people, just like you and me, so long as we are willing to listen, surrender, and follow. There is absolutely nothing special about me. I merely gave the Holy Spirit space in me to do what He does best.

I prayed that my pain would be used to help just one other person. That's all I wanted. I needed there to be a purpose in my pain. I have since received hundreds of messages, emails, and letters telling me about how my story has impacted their lives. I felt a strong sense of purpose in helping other people going through their own grief. I became passionate about it and prayed for discernment about how I could use this gift God has given me to help others.

We are all going to face grief and pain in our lives, that is promised. But when it happens to us, we have a choice about how we are going to respond to it. None of us are victims to our circumstances. Our stories are constantly refining us and giving us the opportunity to grow in our relationship with Jesus, if we let them. I believe God when He says He will restore and renew what was taken and that it will be even more amazing because I'm watching Him do it in my life right now.

Redemption, in a biblical sense, is when God takes something or someone that is broken or corrupt and restores it back to its original state and purpose. It can be easy for us to see God's redemptive promises in someone else's life and story, but it can be difficult to see it in our own. I was left broken in more ways than one. My heart, my kids, my dreams, my plans, my job, my identity, my self-worth, and my perspective, were all shattered in an instant. I was left with what felt like nothing. But I had seen God work miracles in other people's lives and heard stories of redemption so I had hope that it could be possible for me, too. I'm so grateful for where that trust has led me, what it has taught me, and what it has shown me... to keep holding on and trusting. No matter how far gone you may think you are, you are never beyond the reach of Jesus.

CHAPTER 18:
UNCOMFORTABLE
QUESTIONS

"He will wipe every tear from their eyes. There will be no more death or mourning or crying or pain, for the old order of things has passed away."
Revelation 21:4 (NIV)

Alex and I attended a childbirth education class before having Halle. They talked about labor and delivery, postpartum, and hospital expectations. While the class was helpful to tangibly see what to expect, it didn't prepare either of us for her birth or recovery. I completely zoned out while the nurse teaching the class talked briefly about c-sections because I was so certain I wouldn't have one. After Halle was born, I felt like a fish out of water. I was not prepared for the recovery from a c-section. No one warned me not to sleep in my bed because I would need assistance to get up every two hours to nurse. Laughing and sneezing brought on some of the most intense pain I had ever felt. When people would say something funny, I would consciously think about something sad so I wouldn't laugh and feel the quick sting under my freshly cut open skin. I had no idea that the staples would stay in me for a week. They brought so much discomfort and were a visible reminder of her traumatic birth. No one told me about how when I would catch a glimpse of my body in the mirror I would initially be scared. There were so many things I was unprepared for with my recovery because I never took the time to learn about it because I was so sure it would never happen to me.

Grief *will* happen to every single one of us at some point in this lifetime. Maybe once, maybe a few times. We don't know. However, I was not prepared for grief to strike my life in my twenties.

There were things that Alex and I failed to talk about and establish due to the assumption that we had more time to complete them. We said we would make a will when we were done having kids. That seemed to be the most logical to both of us to make sure that our children were taken care of. I am begging you to create a will or a living will. In it, make sure to include who gets what. One of the biggest reasons families are torn apart after death is trying to decide who gets what based on who they think deserves it more. Do everyone you love in your life a favor, and clearly outline those assets so it is known and there isn't a reason to fight over it. Appoint guardianship for your children and/or pets in the event both parents are gone. Who do you trust to raise your children for you if something were to happen? This is a huge decision and having the conversation with your spouse ahead of time is so important. Detail all financials. Make guidelines for the executor here and the age you want your kids to get their share of the money. This is the other biggest reason families get torn apart. Money was Alex's department, he took care of all of that for me so I never had to. I had no idea what we were paying on most things, and that was extremely naive of me.

We didn't have supplemental life insurance on either of us because we never expected to need it so early on in life. I will tell you that as a teacher, I got $10,000 life insurance for being a part of the union. Alex had $15,000 for his job. Those may seem like big numbers, but when paying for a wake and funeral service, casket, grave vault, and a headstone, those numbers don't help cover more than one of those. That doesn't include a mortgage, student debt, car payments, loans, bills, school, or any other thing you would have to pay for. Please get supplemental life insurance. Life insurance is designed to provide your family with financial security in the event of a tragedy. It is suggested that you take your annual salary and multiply it by 8. Take into consideration adding enough to pay off the big things like mortgage, school loans, cars, funeral expenses, and more.

Now for the uncomfortable conversations. At the moment, these may feel gruesome and uncomfortable, but I promise they are so necessary and would take such a big weight off the living. First, your funeral arrangement. *Do you want to be buried or cremated?* If you want to be buried here are just a few things to consider. *Do you have any casket requests? Is there a specific outfit you wish to be buried in? Where do you want to be buried? Do you want anything special buried with you? If you want to be cremated, do you want to be cremated with anything special to you? Where do you want your ashes spread? Do you still want a headstone or place for family and loved ones to visit? As far as the funeral service goes, are there any specific songs, speakers, dress code, poems, etc that you want followed? If money isn't an issue, do you have a special charity or foundation that friends and family can donate to on your behalf?* I know this sounds like a scary conversation but I promise knowing the answer to some, if not all, of these questions will help so much.

If you are married, here are the things I strongly encourage you to do today! Make sure both of your faces are registered on your face id on your phone and write down entry passwords. This ensures that you are still able to get onto their phone and never lose the precious pictures, videos, and conversations.

I suggest getting a notebook and locking it away in a safe. In that notebook, make a list of all username and passwords for any and all accounts. Any services you pay for, Netflix, Spotify, Amazon Prime, all bills, write it down. You are going to need access to get into every single account you and your spouse have. We all know how frustrating it can be when you cannot get into an account that you need because you can't remember the login information. I would also include all financial account information in this notebook. List out all bank accounts, all businesses with a contact for the best person that can help sort out the details. This was huge for me because I expected Alex to handle all of the finances, and when he passed, I had no idea about any of it! The last thing I would include in this notebook, are your necessity bills. *What bills do you have to keep paying to survive? You want to make sure you have access to all of the essential accounts that you are both added on as joint account holders (not just an authorized user). What is on auto pay and what isn't? Which account does it pull from?*

This certainly isn't everything, but it's a good start to alleviate stress for your loved ones after you pass. It takes the guessing away and has the hard decisions made for them in a time when they are constantly reminding themselves how to breathe. These conversations and decisions are uncomfortable to make but are such a blessing to have.

CHAPTER 19: AN INTENTIONAL LIFE

"He has made everything beautiful in its time."
Ecclesiastes 3:11 (ESV)

Writing a book has never been a dream of mine. I never enjoyed writing papers for classes and sharing my life so vulnerably was never the plan I had for my life. Since losing Alex, writing and sharing vulnerably has been an organic part of my healing journey, and nothing I did could shake the feeling that perhaps God created me specifically for such a time as this. I ended up quitting my job as a teacher to write this book and fully surrender the plans I had for my life. I would've laughed in your face if you would've told me I'd be twenty-eight years old, widowed, with two little kids, leaving teaching and writing a book. What someone once told me is true:

"If God put it on your heart, there's nothing you can do to make it go away."

I found myself in the deepest, darkest valley I have ever been in two years ago. I felt like God went radio silent on me in some moments. I have never felt so alone and so betrayed as I did on June 10th. I can now look back on my story and say with absolute certainty that even when we think God is silent and not hearing our prayers, or working things out for our good, He absolutely is. When God seems most *absent*, He's actually most *active* behind the scenes. I've heard this compared to the analogy of when a baby first learns to walk or swim. Think about when you are helping them, the more steps or strokes they begin to take, the more steps you take away from them. It may seem as though we are backing away and becoming more absent, when in reality we are being strategic and trying to help them build their muscles to become more sturdy. Perhaps, this is what God is doing with us during these moments when He feels distant. He is preparing us for something we never could've imagined for ourselves—this book for example.

Leaving my job as a teacher was a terrifying experience filled with so much uncertainty. Worry filled my mind when I thought about how to provide for my kids and myself, and the school's ability to find a replacement for me. How was the community going to react to my decision? What were people going to think about me leaving the only job I had ever known for the past seven years? The comfort of teaching had been my safe place for so long, yet it did not fill my soul. While I adored my colleagues, boss, and the students I taught, the stress of the job had drained me. I felt like I wasn't living out my true purpose in life and that my days were passing in a blur of safety and familiarity. I prayed for guidance, discernment, and peace-of-mind regarding my decision. I knew I had to take this leap of faith and pursue my true calling, even though it meant leaving behind the security of my job. I have found fulfillment and purpose beyond measure and a newfound sense of peace has filled my soul. The feeling of overwhelming stress and anxiety no longer follows me around. I have poured my heart into my work and am more intentional in every moment with my kids. Each day that passes reminds me that I made the right decision. But this journey wouldn't have been possible if I hadn't first surrendered and trusted the author of my story. Embracing my future wasn't easy, but it was definitely worth it.

I have learned not to judge God's faithfulness by how easy or how well things are going. The Bible promises us that suffering is inevitable, but rest assured that He is always faithful. Instead of being discouraged by this truth, use it as encouragement to start living the life you want right now. Stop waiting, stop trying to find the perfect time, and do the thing that has been placed on your heart and isn't going away. The world we live in is volatile, with no assurances. Everything can change in the blink of an eye. Tell the people who mean the most to you that you love them. Help others however you can and find Jesus in your life. Because when suffering happens, He is our only hope of getting through another day. When we experience loss and we walk with Christ in that, what loss begins to do is eliminate how tethered we are to this world. It eliminates fear and fear is a driving force in our society. Fear robs so much from us and we're searching for something that only God can provide. While we are all trying our best in our daily lives to make a positive impact on the world, it's important to reflect on how we want to be remembered. Reminding ourselves of this can help shift our perspective and think about our long term goals.

We currently are still living in the same house where Alex proposed, we brought our dog home, told my family we were expecting, brought both of our babies home from the hospital, and so much more. This is the last place I saw my husband, and I feel him the most. Gunner is buried in our yard. I love the yard and there are so many pieces of him here, but I finally feel ready to move. Alex and I had big plans and a vision for how we were going to transform this house into our forever home. It's an old, country house that needs a lot of work, but we wanted to do that together. The kitchen is so small that we couldn't be in there at the same time. He wanted to open it up and add in windows for me to watch the beautiful sunset every night. There is only one bathroom. We needed the current one moved, and more added in for our growing family. We wanted another baby together. We planned on turning part of the playroom and the screened in porch into the fourth bedroom. At times it's painful looking around at the

house and seeing it remain exactly the same after two years, when we talked about beginning the renovations just weeks before the accident. I can't tell you exactly when we will move, but I know that this house was meant for the four of us, not the three of us.

I am confident that there is a purpose in our pain. God never allows us to suffer without a purpose in mind. God is preparing you for a greater assignment and is using your pain as a training ground for it. Think about a dark room that develops photographs. Sometimes we find ourselves in a dark room, and if we are exposed to the light too early, it ruins the picture. God is developing each and every one of us in our own unique ways to imprint His plan on our lives. He knows what we never could. My hope in being open and honest about my pain and surrendering is that it reveals just how radically our God wants to work in all of our lives, especially when we're suffering. Trusting in God through my greatest heartbreak was not easy by any means. It was a conscious choice that I had to make daily, sometimes several times each day. It came with setbacks, disappointments, and questions. But it also came with the most unexplainable peace, joy, and purpose that I have ever experienced. Trusting in God doesn't guarantee a quick fix to your problems or instant healing for your heartaches, but it can bring about a sense of peace and hope that surpasses understanding. The rewards of trusting in God may not always be tangible or immediate, but they are said to be the sweetest of all - a deep sense of inner strength, resilience, and comfort that can help you navigate through life's challenges with grace. I would've never chosen this story for my life in a million years, and I hate that heartache and loss may be part of your story, too, but take heart and know that our God chose you, will never forsake you, and is working to make all things new. You are fully known and loved by Him.

I am not who I was two years ago. Losing Alex has changed every part of me, but loving Alex made me better from the moment I met him. Because of who he was and how he lived, he continues to positively impact people's lives, even strangers. He always found a way to make you feel comfortable and heard. He loved hard and wasn't afraid to show his affection. He always dreamed big and encouraged those around him to do the same. Anytime I had an idea that seemed far-fetched or unrealistic, Alex always downplayed it and assured me that I could do it with ease. I never got the chance to tell him my crazy idea of writing a book, but I know he would've encouraged me to do it and would have been so proud. He is forever reminding us all to listen a little more, hug a little tighter, and talk a little longer. I urge you not to wait for something tragic to happen to begin living your life with more intentionality and purpose. Love your people hard, let go of the small things, and remember that eternity is the goal.

EPILOGUE: PRACTICALLY SPEAKING

"But we do not want to be uninformed, brothers and sisters, about those who have died, so that you may not grieve as others do who have no hope. For since we believe that Jesus died and rose again, even so, through Jesus, God will bring with him those who have died."
1 Thessalonians 4:13-14 (NRSV)

Once the initial shock settled down, I remember feeling angry that the funeral home didn't give me an explicit packet with different options I could do before my husband was locked in a casket and buried six feet below the ground. I was so numb that I wasn't thinking about different things I could do with his fingerprint and such. It wasn't until I saw other widows who have gone before me share what they did that got me thinking about how naive and unaware I was about death altogether.

There are so many different things that you can do to honor your loved one and I'm sure I won't be able to name all of them. I can only share what I wish I had done differently.

Fingerprint: I love that when you run your fingers across, you feel the bumps of their unique fingerprint.
- Jewelry (bracelet, ring, necklace, pendants, lockets, cufflinks, lapel pins, tie tacks)
- Keepsakes (pocketknife, ornament, keychain, bookmark, teddy bear, cigar cutter, money clip, framed memorial plaque, lighter)

Plaster hand molding: The molding really does a great job of capturing the details, years, wear and tear, every wrinkle, and every crevice is forever tangible.
- Their individual hand
- Holding hands with them

Flowers: With the abundance of flowers here are some meaningful ways to use them instead of throwing them away.
- Preserve them by hanging upside down.
- Pressed flower artwork (turns out so beautiful)
- Pull off petals and send them in to be turned into:
  - Jewelry

- Ornaments
- Bookmarks
- Candles
- Beads

Clothing: You're left with every single piece of clothing they ever bought. There is so much you can do with it, but I did a little bit of all of these.

- Donate them
- Keep some for yourself to continue wearing
- Keep some for your kids to wear in the future
- Turn clothing into:
  - Teddy bears
  - Pillows
  - Clothes to fit your kids
  - Quilts/blankets

Other ideas:

- Frame letters they wrote to you
- Turn their letters into a book
- Tattoo in their handwriting
- Jewelry (necklace, bracelet, ring) in their handwriting
  - If cremated, you can use their ashes to be turned into jewelry as well.
- Wear Felicity is a brand that puts a picture inside a piece of jewelry that you can look at whenever you want.

Honoring our loved ones goes so much deeper

than tangible objects and gifts. It's actively choosing that if you can no longer live your life *with* them, that you will live life *for* them.

Forever missing you, and always loving you, Alex Paulsen.

ACKNOWLEDGMENTS

<u>Manda Carpenter</u>
My writing coach who walked me through every single step of this process. This book would not be possible without her encouragement, tough love, and guidance.

<u>Allie Baughman</u>
For doing all the grammar edits on this book and bringing my vision for the cover to life. I couldn't have done it without your help and kind words of encouragement.

<u>Emily Cruz</u>
For helping me learn how to format and upload my book to be able to sell it.

<u>My family - especially Aimee & Anita</u>
My family was thrilled for me when I told them I was leaving my job as a teacher and wanted to write a book. They sent messages of encouragement, prayed for me, helped me write parts of the book, and answered constant text messages at all hours of the day and night. Saying they are my biggest supporters would be an understatement.

<u>Cloey Weber</u>
My best friend, who always believes in me and helps me reach my goals while fiercely loving my family. She

always points me toward what is most important and helped me remain true to myself throughout this process.

Connor & his family
Connor helped me look past my doubts and made me realize I am capable of doing hard things. He helped me focus on the end goal instead of all the obstacles on the way to getting there. Connor's entire family has been rooting for me and encouraging me throughout the entire process. Their genuine excitement for me is contagious.

Andy Huette
My pastor who still checks in on me and prays for and with me often. Whether he knows it or not, he has helped me keep going these past two years in so many ways. His check-ins and hard conversations are always needed and appreciated.

Lanette & Ashley
For watching and loving on my kids during the day so that I was able to get this book done.

Mike & Ashley Bell
For being the driving factors behind gaining the confidence to quit my job and follow my heart to write a book. Also for continuing to check-in and provide for my family.

Caitlin & Luke Bachtold
For capturing all of our family photos throughout the
years including almost all of the pictures you see in this
book.

Paul & Sharlene Bullard
For raising the man of my dreams and giving me the gift
of Alex.

To every single person who has prayed for me, cried with
me, listened to me, and hoped with me through this
valley: Thank you will never feel like quite enough.

ABOUT THE AUTHOR

Kellie was raised in the suburbs of Chicago and after graduating college, she married Alex in 2018 and moved to central Illinois. She got her bachelor's degree in Elementary Education and taught in the classroom for seven years. They had two children, one girl and one boy, and they were living out a real-life fairytale on their farm in the country.

In 2021, Alex was in a tragic car accident. Overnight, at 26 years old, Kellie became a widow and single mom to their two year old daughter and seven week old son. After losing her husband, Kellie quit her job to heal, which led her to write and share her grieving journey online. Although she wouldn't have chosen this for her life, she has learned to fully surrender to God and recognize how present He is, even in the valleys.

By openly sharing her story, Kellie not only found solace for herself but also became passionate about leading others through their own healing process.

Made in the USA
Middletown, DE
26 September 2024

61468542R00109